S0-ASN-405

To Mom and Dad
and to
Ed, Warren, and Carol
We talked, and I learned so much.

M.A.H.

Dedicated to friends and colleagues who have lent their support and encouragement throughout the years, especially:

Joanna Nicholson
Bena Kallick
June Gould
Alice Kelly
Janet Horowitz
Ellen Goldstein
Lynn Sprague
Dorrie Henninger
Debby Dixler
Mary Mayhew
and
Lisa Durkin

K.F.

# THINK IT THROUGH

Developing thinking skills with young children

by
Martha A. Hayes
and
Kathy Faggella

Art by
Kathy Faggella

**FIRST TEACHER PRESS**
First Teacher, Inc./Bridgeport, CT

ISBN 0-9615005-2-2

Library of Congress Catalog Card Number 86-82298

Design by Alice Cooke, A to Z Design, NYC

Cover Design by Alice Cooke; Illustration by Debby Dixler

Edited by Lisa Lyons Durkin

Associate Editor: Francesca DeMaria

Editorial Assistant: Kathleen Hyson

Technical Assistant: Michael Bashar

Manufactured in the United States of America.

Published by First Teacher Press, First Teacher, Inc.
P.O. Box 29, 60 Main Street, Bridgeport, CT 06602.

Distributed by: Gryphon House, Inc.
P.O. Box 275
Mt. Ranier, MD 20712

# TABLE OF CONTENTS

# TABLE OF CONTENTS

**CELEBRATIONS**

# WE BELIEVE THAT

- each child should be encouraged to think creatively in order to solve problems.
- each child should have the opportunity to seek solutions to problems and respect should be shown for her solutions.
- each child should learn the process of problem solving in order to be able to apply it to any new situation that she might encounter.
- the thinking skills a child uses to solve a problem are more important than the final solution she proposes.
- each child should be given the opportunity to experience thinking skills concretely at first in order to then do abstract thinking.
- each child needs to have the opportunity to talk through her thinking as she discusses the problem with other children and adults.
- through experience each child can learn which solutions are better than others.
- each child should gain a feeling of satisfaction and self confidence from solving problems constructively.

# OUR PHILOSOPHY

***"Early childhood classrooms should provide many reasoning and problem-solving opportunities for children."***

Newborn babies come into this world with few instincts. Other than a few basic fears and the ability to suck, infants start off life without much help. However, humans have the ability to think and to reason. This process starts at the moment of birth. Babies can use their senses of sight, hearing, taste, touch, and smell to begin to understand and later control their world.

Infants are able to use their observations and collections of sensations to help satisfy their basic needs. Their thinking powers enable them to find ways to communicate their desires in order to be fed when hungry, put to bed when tired, and so on. In a very basic sense, babies have learned to solve their first problems.

Problem solving is a skill that should be practiced continually from infancy on. Children need to learn how and where to acquire knowledge and then how to use the knowledge to solve problems. Parents provide opportunities, and so do you, their teacher. Early childhood classrooms should make available many experiences and situations where children can reason and solve problems on their own.

Everyday we are teaching and helping our children learn thinking and problem-solving skills. You are already providing the situations and opportunities to get them to reason on their own. We believe that children can form solutions to any problems that they might encounter if they have been taught and are given the opportunity to practice problem-solving skills.

We believe that this process can be taught by first having children learn skills involved in problem solving: observing details, making comparisons, classifying, placing things in sequence, understanding cause and effect, making inferences, and predicting outcomes. We believe that children must learn these skills at first through concrete experiences before they can proceed to abstractions.

We also feel that children need to talk through solutions and check them out with their friends and classmates under the attention of a caring adult. Eventually, we know that children will be able to distinguish the fact that some solutions are better than others. With practice at verbalizing and working out situations, children will find problem solving and thinking a satisfying task that will, in the end, enhance their feelings of competence and self-esteem.

# CHILDREN & THINKING

**To the young child, thinking is:**

- noting details
- making comparisons
- classifying
- noting sequence
- understanding cause and effect
- making inferences
- predicting outcomes

**Thinking is noting details:**

When children note details with their eyes, they can name items and give descriptions that also may include adjectives involving other senses—hearing, smell, touch, and taste. Certain questions or directions will encourage children to note details.

- "What is the name of this object?"
- "What do you think this is called?"
- "Tell about what you see."
- "What colors do you see?"
- "What size do you think it is?"
- "Tell something about it after you touch (taste, listen to, smell) it."

**Thinking is making comparisons:**

When children make comparisons, they are looking at two or more things and making decisions concerning the similarities and differences. The items may be exactly alike or have parts that are similar. Children will need to note details in order to make comparisions. Certain questions or directions will encourage children to make comparisons.

- "Do these things look the same or are they different from each other?"
- "What makes these objects look alike?"
- "Tell what you think is the same about the things you are looking at."
- "Is this object bigger or smaller than this other object?"

**Thinking is classifying:**

When children classify, they are able to sort objects, people, events, and ideas into groups to which they can belong. The sorting is possible because the members of each group have similar characteristics or uses. As children sort, they are noting details and making comparisons. Certain questions or directions will encourage children to classify.

- "Pick out all the objects that are (red)."
- "What is the name of the group to which all these objects belong?"
- "What is alike about all of these items?"

**Thinking is noting sequence:**

When children note sequence, they are describing the order in which a series of events occurred or telling about the order of a sequentially arranged pattern. That pattern also may include noting the degrees of differences in a single concept such as temperature, size, or shading. Children need to be familiar with the words used to describe each type of order. Certain questions or directions will encourage children to note sequence.

- "What happened first, next, and last?"
- "Tell what color object comes next in this pattern."
- "In what order do you put on your shoes and socks?"
- "Which day was the coldest? On which day did you feel the warmest?"

**Thinking is understanding cause and effect:**

When children are able to figure out either the cause or the effect of an action or an event, they are able to understand "why" it happened or "what" will happen. They begin to realize that there are reactions or results for everything that occurs. Certain questions or directions will encourage children to think about and understand cause and effect.

- "Tell why you think this happened."
- "What do you think caused that result?"
- "Tell what will occur if you do this."

**Thinking is making inferences:**

When children make inferences about an event, person, or situation, they are making a guess about implied details or they are filling in the gaps of information that are not stated. In order for children to "guess" correctly, they need to have had some background of experiences with the concepts being discussed. Certain questions or directions will encourage children to make inferences.

- "If you are told to open a door, what are all the things that you have to do?"
- "Tell why you think the little bear is unhappy when Goldilocks eats his porridge."
- "If you are told to cut out a picture, what steps must you remember to do?"

**Thinking is predicting outcomes:**

When children predict the outcome of a situation, they use the skills of sequencing, understanding cause and effect, and making inferences about what happened in order to figure out or "guess" the possible ending or outcome. Certain questions or directions will encourage children to predict outcomes.

- "Tell what you think will happen next."
- "What will occur at the end if the following events take place?"

# HOW TO USE THIS BOOK

***"Typical early childhood themes are springboards for practicing thinking skills."***

*Think It Through* is a guide that shows you how to enhance the thinking skills of the children you teach. We have provided suggested activities and projects that demonstrate typical early childhood themes. We show how these themes can be used as springboards for practicing skills for problem solving and for creative thinking. In most of these, children are working with real-life, concrete materials. You can use the suggestions as written or adapt them to your own situations.

Each chapter contains activities that enhance the specific skills of noting details, making comparisons, classifying, noting sequence, understanding cause and effect, making inferences, and predicting outcomes. There are two project pages in a chapter that list, step-by-step, activities to do with children that reinforce the skills on the previous pages. There is a picture page or pages in each chapter that can be reproduced and given to children. These pages are participatory pages in that they require the children to do something on them using certain thinking skills. Finally, each chapter closes with a creative thinking page. These pages suggest a number of short activities that give children chances to brainstorm solutions to problems and think through different types of situations.

*Think It Through* can serve as a catalyst for your class. Our suggested activities were written to benefit most children. You, however, will want to personalize the problem-solving situations to meet the needs of the children in your particular groups. Use this book to assist you in planning other experiences that will enable children to practice the same skills. Develop your own problem-solving situations.

On the project pages, the directions given refer to the child. We use the term "adult" when a task is too difficult or too dangerous for a young child to do alone. However, you must be the final judge of what your child can do. Remember that safety is always the major concern.

# PRE-READING SKILLS HIGHLIGHTED IN THINKING PROJECTS

| | Cause and Effect | Classification | Creative Thinking | Comparison | Details | Following Directions | Inference | Math | Opposites | Patterning | Predicting Outcomes | Relationships -Color | Relationships -Place | Relationships -Shapes | Sequence |
|---|---|---|---|---|---|---|---|---|---|---|---|---|---|---|---|
| Paper Plate Face (page 29) | | | X | | X | X | | | | | X | | | | |
| Love Thermometer (31) | | X | X | | | | | X | | | | | | | X |
| Self-Measuring Tools (32) | | | X | | X | | X | X | | | | | | | |
| Comparative Growth Chart (33) | | | X | | | | X | X | | | | | | | |
| The Leafy Sort (37) | | X | X | X | X | | | X | X | | X | | X | | |
| Great Grapes (39) | X | | | X | | X | X | | X | | | | | X | X |
| A Story for Fall (41) | X | X | | X | X | | | | X | | | | | X | X |
| Hot—Cold Hands (43) | X | X | X | | | | X | X | X | | | | | | X |
| Freezing Fun (45) | X | | | X | X | X | X | | X | | | | | X | X |
| This is Me (47) | X | X | | X | X | | | | X | | | X | | X | |
| Bugs, Bugs, Bugs...(49) | | | | X | X | X | | | | | | | X | | X |
| Grassy Eggheads (51) | X | X | | X | X | X | | | X | | | | | X | X |
| Spring Scavenger Hunt (53) | | X | X | X | X | | | | X | | | X | | | |
| Poster Word (55) | | | | X | X | X | | | | X | | | | | X |
| Sand Storytellers (57) | X | | | X | X | | | | X | | | | | X | X |
| A Seasonal Scene (58–59) | X | X | | X | X | X | | | X | | | X | | X | X |
| Picture Word Book (63) | | X | X | X | X | X | | | | | | | | | X |
| What Happens When (65) | X | | | X | X | | | | X | | | | | | |
| Words Alive! (66) | | X | X | X | | | | | X | | | X | | | |
| Where Is My Little Dog Going? (67) | | | | X | X | X | | | | | | X | | | |
| Scrap Counting Poster (71) | | | | X | X | X | X | | | X | | | | | X |
| Spicy Cooked Applesauce (73) | X | | | | X | X | X | | X | | | | | X | X |
| Finish the Pattern (74) | | | | | X | X | | | | X | | | X | | X |
| Get the Beat (75) | | | | | X | | | | | X | | | | | X |

# PRE-READING SKILLS HIGHLIGHTED IN THINKING PROJECTS

| | Cause and Effect | Classification | Creative Thinking | Comparison | Details | Following Directions | Inference | Math | Opposites | Patterning | Predicting Outcomes | Relationships -Color | Relationships -Place | Relationships -Shapes | Sequence |
|---|---|---|---|---|---|---|---|---|---|---|---|---|---|---|---|
| Play Dough Beads (79) | X | | | | X | X | | | | X | X | | | | X |
| Colors of My Rainbow (81) | X | | | | X | X | X | | | | | X | | | |
| The Fruit Market (82–83) | | X | X | | X | | | | | | | X | | X | |
| Peanut Butter (87) | | | | X | | X | | | | | X | | | | |
| Musical Cups (89) | X | | | | X | X | | | | | | | | | X |
| City Senses (90–91) | X | X | X | X | X | | X | | | | | | X | | |
| Shapely Books (95) | | X | X | X | X | X | | | X | | | | | X | |
| Humpty Dumpty Puzzle (97) | | | | X | X | X | | X | | | | | | X | |
| Story Cards (98–99) | X | | | X | X | | X | | | X | X | | X | | X |
| Hidden Treasures (103) | X | | | X | X | X | X | | | | X | | | | X |
| Pillow Case Costume (105) | | | | X | X | | | | | | | | | | X |
| Put Yourself in the Picture (106–107) | X | | | X | X | | X | | | | X | | X | | X |

# GETTING READY

As with any good teaching, preparation and organization are very important. When planning to emphasize thinking skills, you must consider:

- the space you will be using;
- the general equipment needed;
- the specific equipment needed;
- safety and health rules;
- how you and the children will participate in the process of problem solving and creative thinking.

Following are some suggestions of materials that can be used to encourage children to practice thinking ideas through and to solve problems creatively. Remember to make the most of what is readily available to you and to adapt ideas to your own particular situations.

# LANGUAGE DEVELOPMENT

***"It is important for all children to use language and to increase their knowledge about words."***

Language development is closely linked to thinking skills. Children need to increase their vocabularies and to know the meanings of the new words, so they can explain what and how they are thinking. In the preschool years, they should be seeing concrete or pictorial representations of as many of those words as possible. In each area of the room, pictures, posters, or drawings will aid vocabulary growth. Then, nearby where you have circletime, you will want to keep other props that will encourage them to tell stories, "read" words aloud, listen to poetry, put on plays, and discuss ideas.

***"Encourage children to learn about their language by letting them talk."***

Here are items that can be used as props for storytelling and for language development.

- flannelboard
- small paper figures
- dress-up clothes
- storytelling records
- bulletin boards
- fingerplays
- number charts
- posters
- lapboard
- felt figures
- wordless books
- concept pictures
- dolls and puppets
- color charts
- ABC cards
- language experience charts

***"Encourage children to verbalize concepts and to enter into discussions."***

■ Children can begin by naming objects and describing them, using different senses.
■ As children tell folk and fairy tales using the flannelboard and figures, the listeners can compare their versions with others they have heard.
■ Looking for pictures concerning a specific topic that they can discuss and place on a bulletin board encourages children to classify.
■ Children gain a better understanding of the sequence of events as they retell what happened in a familiar story.
■ Children can discuss "why" different characters in a wordless book act as they do and "what" is the result of their actions.
■ When children explain your directions in more detail, it helps them fill in some gaps and make inferences about what they are to do.
■ Children can begin stories and just before they reach the conclusion, ask others to predict what they think will happen next.

# BOOK CORNER

***"Have a special time when children can look at books and talk about what they have seen."***

Keep copies of favorite, familiar books on shelves where children can "read" them whenever they like. Bring in concept books as you and the children are discussing specific subjects. Use some of those books as you are introducing concepts. Send children to the library shelves to find books that will answer specific questions. Talk about "make-believe" stories and books that show factual details. Let children discuss different types of illustrations. You can help children make up their own books or stories.

Make the book corner a place where children can relax and look at books. You may want to have pillows on the floor, book covers, or stuffed story characters to entice children to look at special books or cassettes or records of stories to which they can listen.

***"A librarian can help you find books on whatever subject you need."***

Below are subject groups of books that you may want to have on hand all the time in your room. Specific titles for these and for other concept books are listed in reference books at your local library.

- nursery rhyme books
- wordless books
- number books
- books about people and careers
- holiday books
- books about colors
- fairy tale books
- ABC books
- poetry books
- books about animals
- books about transportation
- books with science facts
- books about families

***"Books are important learning and entertainment tools."***

Give children many opportunities to look at and listen to the stories found in books. Then, add to their enjoyment by letting them talk about what they have seen and heard.

- Discussing the illustrations allows children to note details.
- Many concept books discuss and show likenesses and differences so children can make visual comparisons.
- Since books are written around certain concepts, children can see objects, animals, or persons that belong together as a group.
- All different types of sequential order can be portrayed in books, such as ABC's, numbers, colors of the rainbow, time changes, and story events.
- As children listen to fictional stories and some nonfictional ones, they will be able to sense both the causes and the results of many events.
- Books give children lots of background information so that it is easier for them to make inferences—they are better able to back up their guesses with proof.
- Good listeners will be able to guess outcomes if you stop in the middle of stories and let them decide what the characters will do next.

# DRAMATIC PLAY AREA

***"Dramatic play situations allow for lots of problem solving."***

Opportunities for different types of dramatic play should occur around the classroom and outside. As children "pretend," all sorts of problem-solving possibilities appear. One important aspect of dramatic play is the interaction between the children without a great deal of direction by an adult. The children will think up problems, and then they will suggest and evaluate different solutions or results. Some areas should be available for children to use each day; others may be developed when certain units have been emphasized.

Pretending can take place in the housekeeping area, where block building occurs, in the garden, where the wheel toys are, at the water or sand table, with dress-up clothes, when the children are setting up a supermarket, and so on.

***"Props will add realism to the dramatic play and perhaps will suggest possible solutions to problems."***

The size of your room will determine the amount of space devoted to each one of the dramatic play areas and whether the materials are out all the time or stored away until requested. You might want to introduce children to some of the following objects so they will know what is available and ways that each may be used.

- tables and chairs
- beds
- dolls and stuffed animals
- blocks
- dishes
- scraps of wood
- rakes
- scoops
- buckets and shovels
- scarves
- empty containers
- stove
- pots and pans
- clothing
- toy zoo animals
- tools
- scraps of materials
- hoes
- buckets
- tricycles
- shoe boxes
- sieves and colanders

***"It is interesting to watch as children come up with different solutions for similar problems."***

■ As children plan what is going to be in their supermarket, their lists include lots of details.

■ Children have a chance to make one-to-one comparisons as they decide how many are "coming to dinner" and they set the table.

■ Sorting the empty boxes on the "supermarket" shelves makes children figure out different ways that the items could be classified.

■ Builders will need to determine the best sequence for building a structure so it will not fall down.

■ Children will be able to figure out causes and their effects as they pretend to plant a garden, observe what occurs in nature and what jobs need to be done, and see the results.

■ As they work together, children will make inferences about what others are expecting them to do.

■ Since children's dramatic play tells a story, they have to think about the outcome of a situation.

# SCIENCE AREA

***"A science corner should have room for displays and experiments."***

A part of the room needs to be set aside for continually changing displays of scientific phenomena that children bring to share or that you wish to introduce to them. The shelves, tables, or countertops should be at a height where children can easily examine the materials. Children can use room there or in other areas such as the art center, water table, or outdoor play yard for conducting experiments.

***"Here is a list of materials you may want to have on hand."***

Some of the essential items that can be kept for displays and for experiments are shown below. Those dealing with living plants or animals can be brought in as the children's interests and your plans dictate.

- mirror
- magnet
- magnifying glass
- rocks
- shells
- fans
- cotton
- tongue depressors
- sponges
- cages
- jars
- containers
- tongs
- marbles
- spools
- tape recorder
- thermometer
- plastic bag and ties
- rocks
- acorns
- pine cones
- tree bark
- seeds
- balloons
- corks
- feathers
- soil
- flour
- soap
- tree branches
- mister
- cornstarch
- styrofoam
- twigs
- fish
- plants

***"Children can gain much knowledge as they work with the materials."***

■ Discussing the different items displayed encourages children to look at the visible details.

■ When children feel objects such as rocks and shells, they can make comparisons.

■ Children are learning about sequence when they figure out the steps in an experiment.

■ As children use fans and sponges at the water table, the effect of "wind" on a floating object becomes obvious.

■ Children can discover that rocks sink and corks float. They are seeing members of two different categories. They may also be able to infer why the rocks sank and the corks did not.

■ Scientific experiment are excellent avenues for letting children predict what they think the results will be.

# MATH AREA

***"Mathematics takes place in all parts of the room."***

You can have a special mathematics corner with visual displays and games and also help children realize that mathematics is used in different places around the room. You will want to show how they measure when they are building with blocks or when they are working in the kitchen. You can demonstrate that you are solving mathematics problems when you count money or see how many children are in attendance. When they pass out paper for art projects, the children are practicing one-to-one correspondence.

***"Here is a list of items to have around the room."***

You will need to decide which items children will have free access to and which ones will be kept for special occasions. Also, you must consider how and when to introduce any game, tool, or concept with which the children are unfamiliar.

- calendar with removable numbers and weather symbols
- dominoes
- rulers
- hand timer
- attribute blocks
- beads and strings
- measuring spoons
- objects to count, such as buttons, rocks, pebbles, craft sticks
- thermometer
- number cards
- two-dimensional geometric shapes
- yardstick
- three-dimensional geometric shapes
- different-sized plastic containers
- clocks

***"Children will need to think problems through when they are doing math."***

■ When children are touching objects as they count to find out how many there are, they are noting details; they should realize that their figures move to a new item each time they say a different number.

■ Setting a table is a good experience for children since they are making one-to-one correspondence and comparing what is at each person's place.

■ Children enjoy looking for objects that are similar in shape to a ball or block—they are classifying shapes.

■ Sequential order plays an important part in mathematics as children count objects, name their ordinal positions, and place them in different pattern arrangements.

■ As children add or subtract objects from a group by moving them together or apart, they are "seeing" the effect of what they did.

■ Often, we give children verbal problems or use many different words to show that we are joining objects together or taking them apart—children have to make a lot of inferences.

■ A lot of mathematics require children to estimate or to guess what they think the answers to problems are—they are using their skill of predicting.

# ART AREA

***"The art area provides excellent places for children to create and to figure out solutions."***

A place should be made available in the classroom where children can work with different art media and create designs, pictures, and three-dimensional objects. Young children need to feel that they can freely experiment with materials after being introduced to them and discover the potential of each type. As they paint, fingerpaint, paste, cut, print, or do other crafts, problems will come up and planning will be necessary. With encouragement, children will find answers and be creative.

***"Here are items that will provide children chances to work with many different media."***

You will need to decide which supplies children can use freely and how each will be stored. You can make up kits with different types of materials, too.

- poster paint
- tempera paint
- brushes
- sponges
- screening
- cookie cutters
- scissors
- construction paper
- string
- smocks or aprons
- old toothbrushes
- combs
- feathers
- cotton
- weaving looms
- fingerpaint
- craft sticks
- muffin tins
- crayons
- clay or play dough
- rolling pin
- glue or paste
- scrap fabrics
- yarn
- easels
- clothesline
- plastic straws
- buttons
- colored markers
- drawing paper

***"It is important that children have opportunities to see what can be done when they handle different art materials."***

■ By introducing colors one at a time, children are able to start noticing details right away.

■ Working with different widths of brushes enables children to make comparisons and decide which one works best for completing a certain part of a picture.

■ Having different media around allows children to classify colors, types of creations that can be made, and different ways the media can be used.

■ As children work to complete a craft project, a collage, or a clay figure, they will either sense the sequential steps that must occur or they will follow the step-by-step directions.

■ In containers, such as muffin tins, where children can mix colors, the effect of adding one color to another can be easily demonstrated.

■ Because of the types of pictures young children draw, lots of inferences must be drawn by both the artist and the viewers.

# MUSIC AREA

***"Music provides children with many opportunities for creativity."***

You will want to set up your room so that children can enjoy singing songs and making music, using real or classmade instruments. Through their singing of already–written songs or by playing along with the piano or a record, children will be learning about the sounds and rhythms of music. They will have a chance to sense the connection between the notes on paper and what is heard. Responding to music with movement also should be encouraged. Allow time and space so the children can create their own music.

***"When children make their own instruments, they learn more about how different tones are caused."***

Some of the musical instruments or noisemakers that you will want to have available in the classroom are listed below. In addition, the list includes objects that may be used by children under your guidance to make their own instruments and objects to use during movement exercises.

- piano
- tape recorder
- triangle
- kazoo
- xylophone
- bells
- aluminum plates
- sticks
- rice kernels
- rocks
- orange juice cans
- paper clips
- string
- wooden blocks
- sand
- oatmeal boxes
- comb
- marbles
- fans
- metal measuring spoons
- record player
- drum
- castanets
- cymbals
- tambourine
- cake pans
- rubber bands
- plastic containers with lids
- paper cups
- waxed paper
- books
- glasses
- wooden spoons
- pot lids
- cake rack
- vegetable grater
- feathers
- scarves
- hoops

***"Children enjoy making up their own music and words."***

■ As children read or play individual notes, they are paying attention to details.

■ Children hear the similarities and differences as they listen to the same music played on different instruments or on records or tapes.

■ Choosing whether the tempo of a song is fast or slow is one way of classifying music.

■ The scale is a sequence of notes that children can learn to recognize.

■ When playing different instruments, children can hear the effect of hitting or blowing into them.

■ Children will be drawing inferences when they are asked to tell how music makes them feel.

# Help Me Think

Dear Parents:

This year we will be encouraging the children to do lots of thinking of their own in all our activities and discussion times. You can help at home by encouraging them to talk about activities they do at school.

You can give your children opportunities to think ideas through by discussing concepts with them. The following are types of questions that will encourage children to use their thinking skills.

- "What is its name? Tell what it looks like."
- "What is alike about these objects? What are the differences?"
- "Tell the name of the group to which all these objects belong. Into what groups would you sort the objects?"
- "In what order did the events in the story take place. What happens first, next, and last?"
- "What do you think made this happen? What will happen if you do this first?"
- "What else do you need to know in order to understand the directions? What do you think has been left out of the story?"
- "Predict or guess what you think will happen next."

Thank you for your help.

____________________

Your child's teacher

# ALL ABOUT ME

# ALL ABOUT ME

**Detail**
*Who Am I? Who Are You?*

One of the most important concepts children learn is body awareness. They learn not only what their bodies look like and feel like, but also what their bodies are capable of doing. Children, in addition, discover how they fit into the surrounding space. They need to be able to identify their own characteristics first so that later on they can make comparisons between themselves and others.

Bring some type of mirror into the room and place it at a level so that children can see themselves in it. Encourage them to give descriptions of themselves as the group is listening so you can become aware of the children's vocabulary development—color of hair and eyes, type of hair, skin coloring, number of fingers, body parts, and so on. Present the materials so that each child is able to make a PAPER PLATE FACE. After the faces have been completed, let other children describe the details of each face and guess the name of the child to whom that face belongs.

**Detail/Comparison**
*What Do I Like?*

You can learn more about the children and their interests at the moment by having them make several *My Favorite* ________ books. Use these books as starting points for discussions. By the questions you ask, children will be noting details and making comparisons. (When the children name their favorite things, they are making some comparisons already.)

Display pieces of construction paper and ask different children to name the colors. Then, ask a question similar to one of the following: "What is your favorite color?"; "Which one do you like best?" After each child has picked a color, provide each with plain white paper and a sheet of construction paper and a crayon of that color. Let them color or cut out objects showing their favorite color. Staple the sheets of paper with their pictures together, so each has a book. You may want to entitle the book *(Child's Name) Favorite Color.*

Similar books can be made about favorite places, clothes, books, and so on. You may need to help children understand what is meant by the word "place."

**Classification/Sequence**
*What Groups Do I Belong To?*

A favorite part of children's lives is their family. By discussing what children think the word "family" means, you will help them clarify their understanding of that category. Many families consist of more than one generation. So, during the children's description, you can discuss the sequential arrangement of families.

Have children draw pictures of what the word "family" means to them or ask them to bring in photographs. Ask them to name everyone in the pictures. You may want to ask questions or discuss such points as the following.

- "When you thinks about the word 'family,' do you also mean your pets?"
- "Can some people be part of your family and still not live at your house?"
- "Is everyone in the family younger or older than you? Which ones are older? How do you know they are older?"

#   

PAPER PLATE FACE

YOU'LL NEED:

crayons

markers

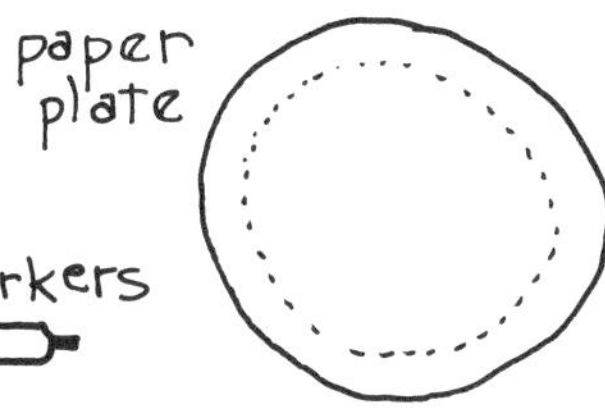
paper plate

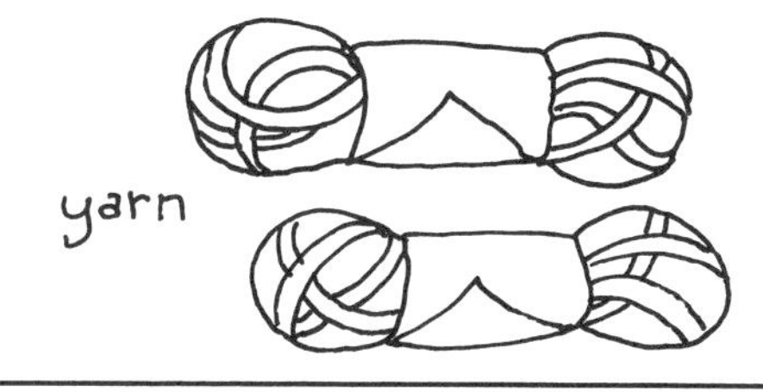
yarn

WHAT TO DO:

1. Children look into a mirror and observe the color of their eyes and their hair. Make some faces, too!

2. With a crayon or marker, color in eyes, nose and mouth.

3. Choose yarn to match hair color and glue in place on paper plate.

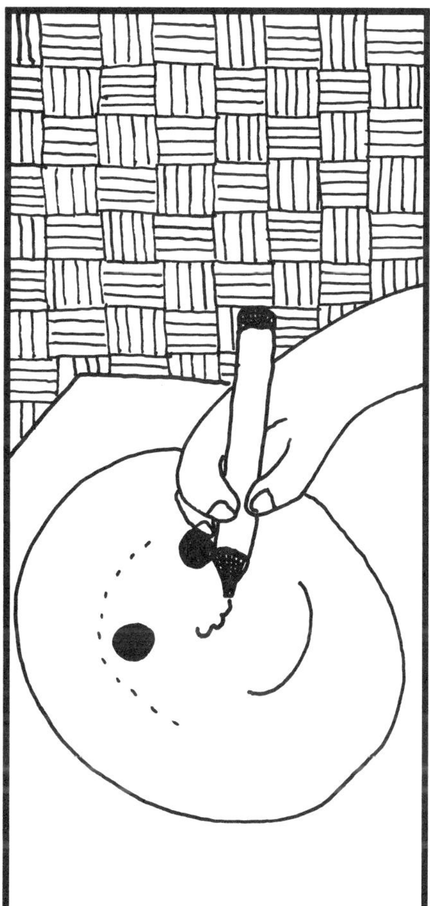

# ALL ABOUT ME

**Cause and Effect**
*Why Do I Feel This Way?*

Help children understand about feelings and what causes them. They need to be able to discuss feelings and the differences between them. Problems often occur because young children don't have the words to express how they feel. They also may have trouble understanding the reasons for feeling a certain way.

Help children make their faces show different types of feelings such as the following: happy, sad, regretful, excited, jittery, and brave. Aid them in thinking of other words that mean the same or nearly the same for each type of feeling. Then, have them think of words that mean the opposite. The LOVE THERMOMETER on page 31 helps show the varying degrees in the meanings of different feeling words. Then, choose a doll or stuffed animal. Explain that this is a make-believe person. Ask a child to make one of the "feeling faces" again as the doll or animal might feel. Let the group name the feeling. Then, ask other children to tell what they think might make the doll or animal feel that way.

**Inference**
*How Do You Know How I Feel?*

Children probably do not realize that facial expressions and body language give many clues as to how a person feels. Since children have to "guess" or make inferences about how someone else feels, it is helpful for them to learn to "read" these clues.

Have children show different emotions by the way they walk or by using their mouths and eyes. Let the rest of the group guess what is being demonstrated. Ask children to tell you the clues that helped them decide what feeling was being shown.

Pick out a familiar folktale or other story in which the characters exhibit various feelings, such as *The Three Bears*. Have children decide in each part of the story how the bears or Goldilocks might feel. Ask them to show the different emotions only with their bodies and facial expressions—the happiness as the bears decide to go for a walk; the sadness when they or Goldilocks discover that the porridge is too hot; the delight of Goldilocks when she likes Baby Bear's chair or bed. Let others guess what is being acted out and what emotion is being shown.

**Predicting Outcomes**
*Playing "Charades" and a Little More*

One consequence that children rarely think about is the effect on others of their reaction to a situation. They also don't consider the event that will occur next. A special type of charades can be played to help them think about the outcomes of their actions and emotions.

Help each child decide first to be either a person or animal. They can choose to be a story character, community helper, imaginary friend, or animal. Have each choose and act out a situation. Ask the group to guess who the situation is about and what the event is. Then, let them decide what the next event might be.

# LOVE THERMOMETER

**YOU'LL NEED:**

one piece heavy cardboard

12"

36"

$52\frac{1}{2}$" long piece of $\frac{1}{2}$" wide sewing elastic

craft knife

red marker

needle and thread

**WHAT TO DO:**

Adult cuts a 3" wide slot 5" down and parallel to the 12" edge.

Adult cuts another 3" wide slot 5" up and parallel to the other 12" edge.

Adult threads the elastic through the two slots so it overlaps $\frac{1}{2}$" in the back. Sew ends together securely.

Turn cardboard to back, move sewn seam section of elastic to bottom slot. Then turn cardboard to the front and color front section of elastic with marker.

Using marker adult or child draws faces and symbols on the front of the Love Thermometer

Children move the red part of the elastic up or down to indicate answers to questions.

"Would you like a nice, cold chocolate ice cream cone on a hot, summer day?"

# Self Measuring Tools

Children tend to relate to everything in terms of themselves—their bodies, senses, egos. Have children measure anything from an insect to the size of a room using fingers, hands and feet. Use the chart opposite to show children how they relate to other growing things.

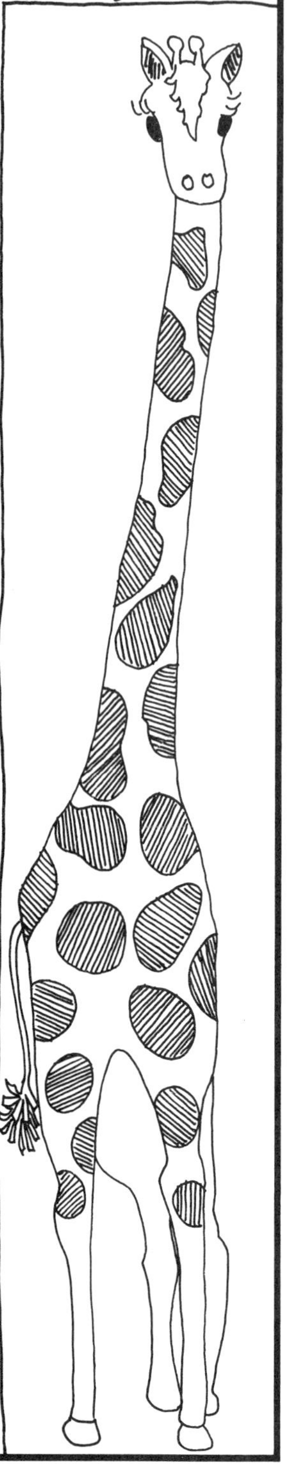

1. Demonstrate where each child's height would be on the chart. Let children draw themselves onto chart.

☆ ☆ ☆ ☆ ☆ ☆ ☆ ☆ ☆ ☆ ☆ ☆ ☆ ☆ ☆ ☆ ☆ ☆ ☆ ☆ ☆ ☆ ☆

2. These insects, the worm and the fish are all drawn actual size. Children can use their hands and fingers, as measuring tools, to compare sizes.

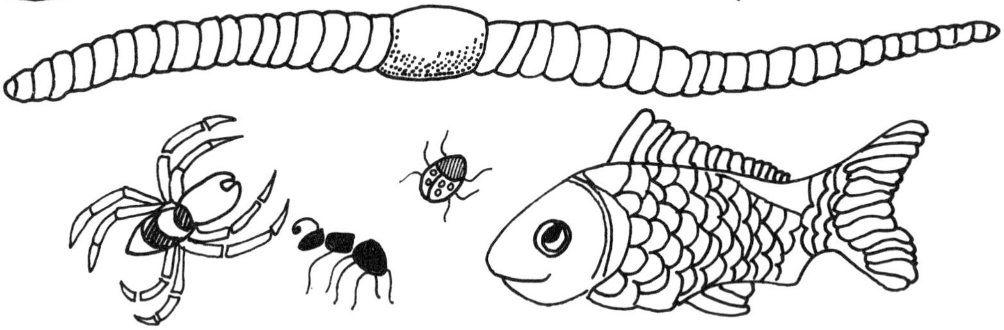

☆ ☆ ☆ ☆ ☆ ☆ ☆ ☆ ☆ ☆ ☆ ☆ ☆ ☆ ☆ ☆ ☆ ☆ ☆ ☆ ☆ ☆ ☆

3. Here are some animals from the Comparative Growth Chart. Children can cut out around each animal shape and arrange the pictures according to height=short to tall.

# Comparative Growth Chart

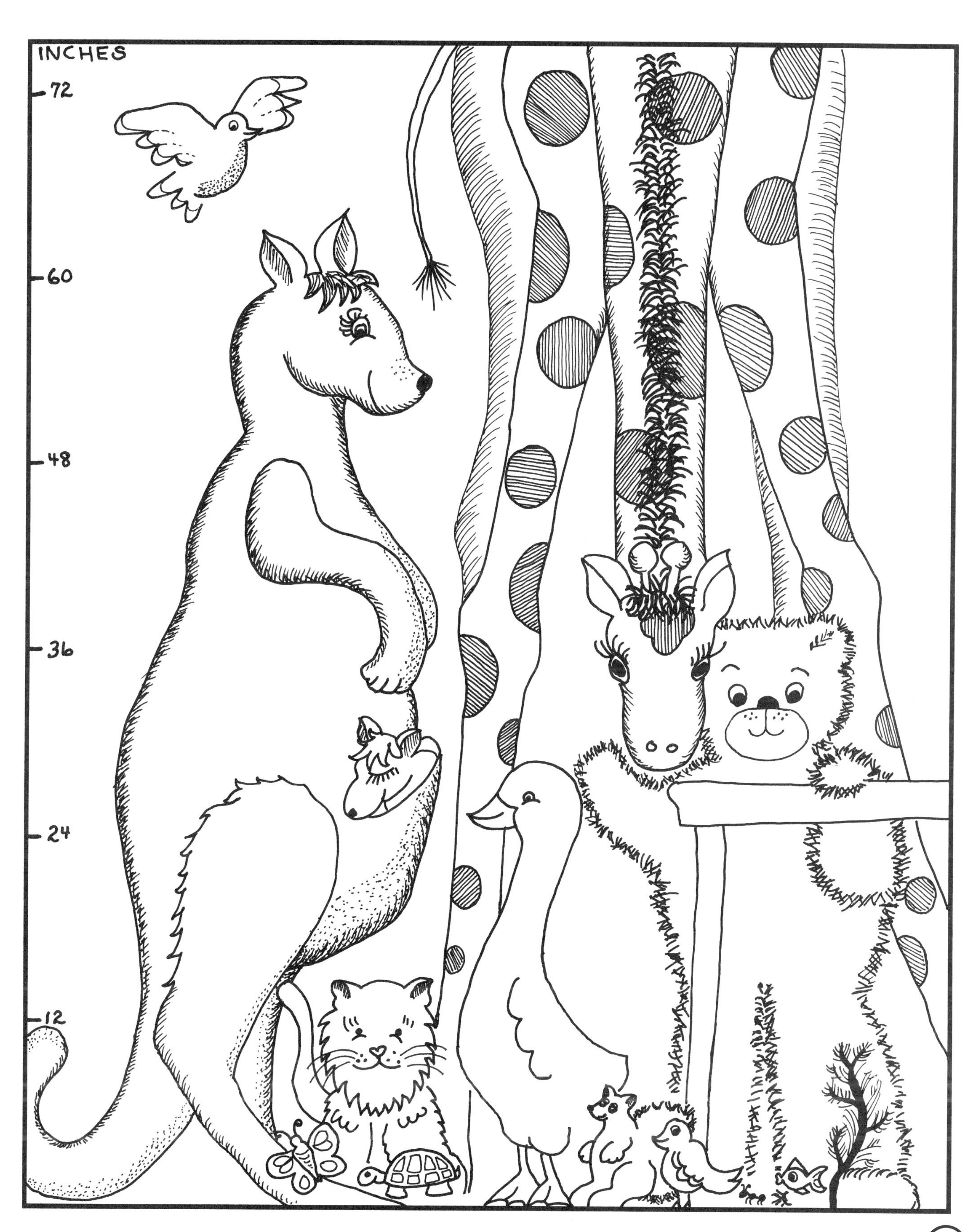

ALL ABOUT ME

# CREATIVE THINKING

Each day, young children have many experiences and they learn from each one. Guide them into more complex, more creative thinking with a well-worded question or provide an activity that will lead them to question and problem solve. Use some of the following suggestions.

Play a game of "What If—." Begin it by posing questions that will help children put themselves in other people or animal's places. You may have to help them understand some concepts suggested.

- "What if you grew 10 feet tall? Where would you live? Where would you eat? Where would you sleep?"
- "What if you were an ant? What food would you eat? What would you use as a bed? What kind of house would you like?"
- What if you were a big elephant? Who would you like to have as friends? What games would you and your friends play?"

Let children decide who or what special thing they would like to be. Have them tell something about that special thing. Suggest that they think about the kinds of questions asked above, if necessary. Then, let others pose questions to them.

Children will more easily talk about "feelings" when questions such as the ones below are posed. Include some points that mention activities that have been frustrating to the children.

- "How would you feel if you had to live in a dollhouse?"
- "How would you feel if you could pick apples from a tall apple tree?"

You can extend a discussion about "feelings" by having children think about what they might do when they feel a certain way. Help them think of what might happen next or what children might do to change that feeling.

- "If a child feels sad, what might that child do?"
- "If a child feels happy, what might that child do?"
- "If a child feels angry, what might that child do?"

Since many young children are not able to understand "why" they feel as they do, they often cannot figure out solutions to help them change their moods. Having a "happy" box in the room may help provide a release for their feelings. Help children develop one. Into the box, you and your children can put "happy things." Children choose "imaginary" items that make them happy and pantomime placing them into the box or each can actually pick out her own "real" item. In either case, it can be a special toy, a person, or a nice memory or a memento of that. Each child may want to tell what she is putting in and why, but they need not. Keep the box on a shelf so children can add new "happy things" whenever they feel like it.

The box comes in handy when a child is sad. Offer the box to the child or let her go to it. Then, she can take out a "happy" thing inserted earlier and think about it. Make sure you add something, too. In that way, you will be helping define "happiness" and show that adults have feelings, also.

# SEASONS

# FALL

**Detail**

*"What's Around" Treasure Hunt*

Provide opportunities for children to look for specific objects outside on a walk. Prepare by picking out examples of objects in the environment such as leaves, acorns, milkweed pods, shiny rocks, pine cones, or bits of tree bark. Be sure that there will be enough objects outside so each child can find the same ones or ones that are similar.

Still in the classroom, show children each special item and have it named. Let them tell one distinctive feature of the object, such as its color or how it feels. Then, go on the hunt. If you are "hunting" outside, carry the examples along. Provide children with paper sacks so that they can bring their treasures back.

**Comparison**

*What Is Alike? What Is Different?*

Here is an activity that allows children to compare objects that have some similar features, but that are different in one or more attribute. Use examples from the treasure hunt above or have children help prepare for this activity by asking them to collect fall items outside.

Hold up two of the same variety of items such as leaves—one that has changed color and one that is still green. Have a child lay one on top of the other so that the group can see that they are the same size or shape. Let other children run their fingers around the edge of each leaf so that they can see and feel the similarities. Then, have children discuss the difference between the two leaves. Show them two different varieties of leaves that are the same color. Continue with other comparisons.

**Classification**

*How Many Ways?*

Let children decide different ways that a collection of fall objects, such as leaves, can be sorted. You may wish to prepare sheets of posterboard as suggested in THE LEAFY SORT ahead of time, but do not show them.

Gather or have children collect examples of the fall object that you want them to sort, such as leaves. Bring in a number of examples of each variety of leaves that show likenesses and differences in color, size, and shape. You may wish to include in their sorting leaves that are still hanging from branches. You may need to tell the first attribute (color or shape) or have children give an obvious similarity by which they can be sorted. Children may begin with color or size since these were presented in the comparison activity. Encourage children to point out examples of each attribute as it is mentioned. If they do not, suggest other attributes. You may want to direct their thinking by holding up two examples that have comparative differences such as maple leaves of two different sizes or two leaves, one of which was just picked from a tree and the other having fallen several days ago.

# THE LEAFY SORT

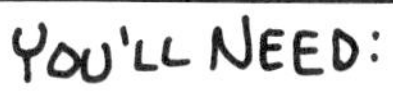

YOU'LL NEED:

posterboard

basket

markers

leaves

WHAT TO DO:

1. Take an outdoor walk and have children pick up many varieties, sizes and colors of leaves.

2. Cut pieces of posterboard into chart sizes. Cut posterboard into 5"x8" pieces for leaf identification.

3. Label, with a marker, each chart or card (as shown below). Then have children find leaves that fit into those categories and place on charts.

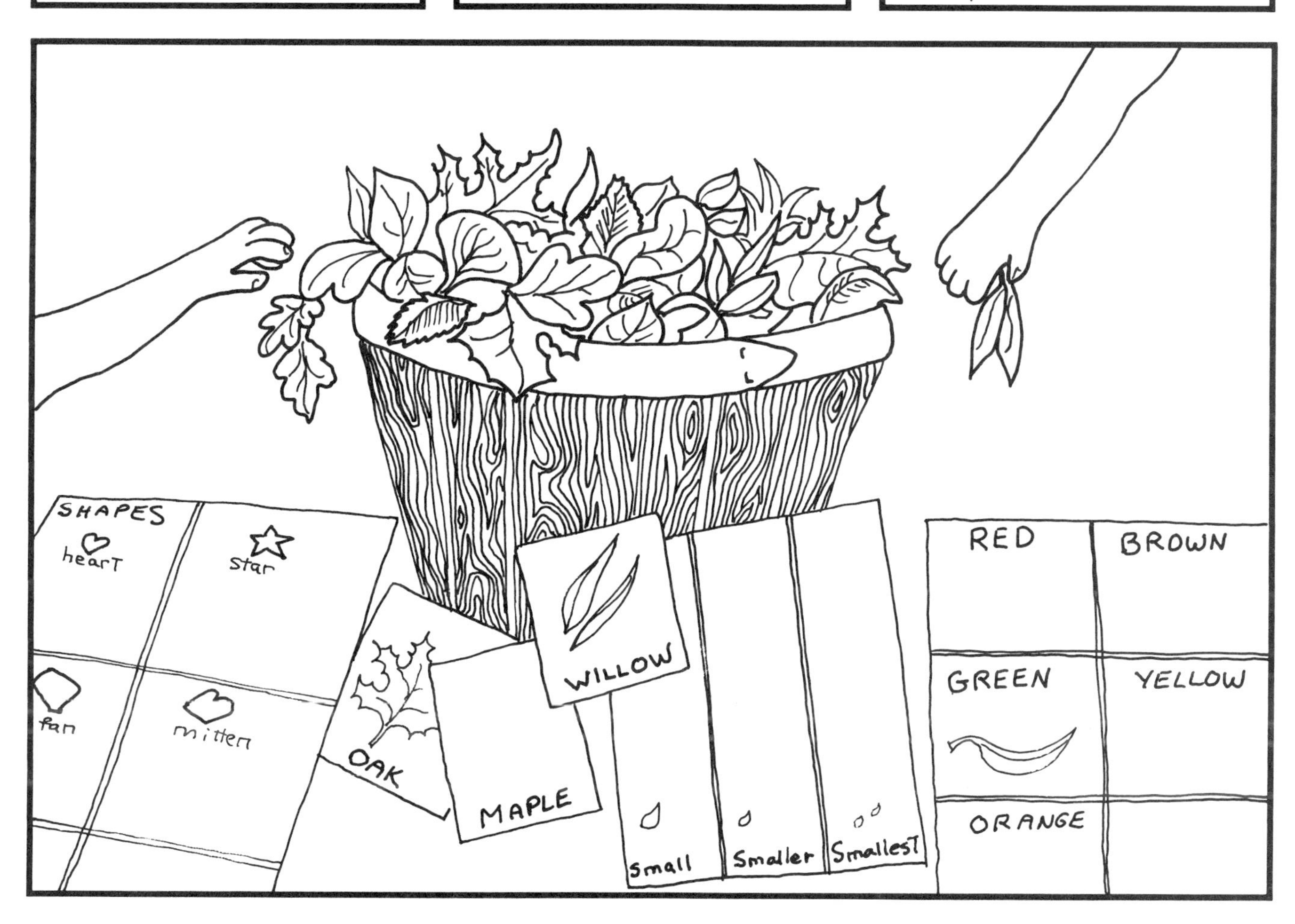

# FALL

**Sequence**
*Let's Think About Order*

This activity will help children understand that sequence can involve gradation from one extreme to its opposite—largest to smallest. (Time sequence in the fall can be shown by the first activity on page 40.)

Find fall objects that are similar except for size—the easiest being four or five leaves that range in size from small to large. Press them flat. Ask children to arrange them in order. Put the first one down on the child's left side so that the child goes from left to right, starting either with the largest or the smallest object. It may help children to "try" the leaves on by laying one leaf over the other to see which one disappears or which one can be seen completely.

**Cause and Effect**
*What Happens and Why*

Here is an opportunity for children to see what happens to objects when certain conditions are changed. You'll need: some green leaves (including spinach), alcohol, water, and various types of covered containers—some clear and some opaque.

Pour alcohol over the spinach leaf so that children can see the green color disappear. They will see that yellow coloring is also an attribute of that leaf.

Place some leaves in a sealed, glass container in which moisture is also present—a jar lid will hold water. Put similar leaves in another container in which no moisture is present. Make the same arrangements in opaque containers. Place the containers on the window ledge in bright sunlight. Each day, let children compare and discuss what is happening to the leaves. Help them think about "why" the changes are occurring— lack of light, lack of water.

Use the GREAT GRAPES experiment to make raisins in order to show more effects of bright sunshine.

**Inference**
*Can You Guess Why?*

Children sometimes have difficulty understanding all the steps involved in experiments and other situations. Let them see all steps in the preparation. You'll need: some green leaves and very dry leaves on branches, some leaves that have already fallen, electric or hand fans.

Display branches of leaves and leaves that have already fallen. Have children present their ideas as to what made the leaves fall. Answers may include the force of the wind, the dryness of the leaves, children picking them, and so on. Let children see how some of their ideas work out. Provide some type of air movement—electric fans or hand motions, so children can see the leaves moving. Point out the branch with the driest leaves on it. Let them keep watching both the green and dry leaves to see which ones fall first. If you have several fans, set them at different speeds.

**Predicting Outcomes**
*What Will Happen Next?*

Ask children to decide what is the first thing they would do if one of the following things happened:

- The weather turned cold and you wanted to go outside.
- The weather turned cold and apples were still on the tree.
- You were a squirrel and nuts started to fall from the trees.

# GREAT GRAPES

**YOU'LL NEED:**

grapes

some of the following:

- 6 oz. chocolate chips
- cinnamon
- 1 tblsp. shortening
- ½ cup peanut butter
- 1 tbsp. honey
- ½ cup salted peanuts
- ½ cup crisp rice cereal
- ½ cup dry milk

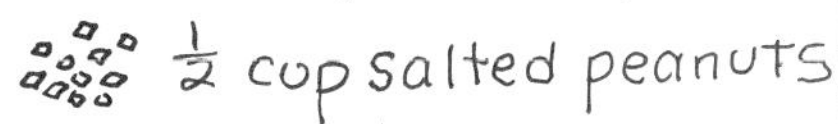

**Make: GRAPE CLUSTERS**

Melt 6oz. chocolate chips and 1 tblsp. shortening in double boiler. Dip tips of small bunch of grapes in chocolate, then in chopped nuts or crisp rice cereal

**Make: Frozen TREATS**

Pull grapes off bunch and place on baking sheet. Freeze until hard. Eat partially frozen.

**Make: RAISINS**

Wash a bunch of green grapes. Pat dry. Place in a basket, in a sunny spot, for one week.

**Make: Grape TREASURES**

Combine ½ cup peanut butter with ½ cup dry milk powder, one tblsp. honey and dash of cinnamon. Mix well. Form mixture around individual grapes to make balls about 1" thick. Roll each ball in ½ cup chopped, salted peanuts. Chill Grape Treasures for best eating.

**WHAT TO DO:**

Obtain grapes from a store or, better yet, right from the vine.

Make some of the above suggested recipes.

Have children brainstorm more ideas for using grapes.

## FALL

# CREATIVE THINKING

So that children can make a link between activities, seasonal changes, and "time," have them make a "Countdown to Fall" chain that starts several weeks before the beginning of fall. On each link, you may wish to suggest or have them tell one activity to do to prepare for the changing of summer to fall. A second way to use the chain is to have children show what sign of fall's coming they have discovered each day. They may want to suspend on one link the first red leaf, a picture of a migrating goose, or an acorn.

Trace the outlines of fall items on the bottom of a shirt box. Scatter the items around the room as children watch. Show them the outlines. Have children choose an outline, find the item that they think fits there, and try matching it to the outline.

Bring in real leaves or have children make pretend ones. Then, have them use the leaves to make a leaf house. Let them decide what rooms to include, how big each should be, what entrances or other openings are needed, and what will be placed in each room.

Bring in different fruits and vegetables that are harvested in the fall. Let children guess or demonstrate how each type of food will be picked.

Let children decide which animal that they would like to be. Ask them to think about what that animal might do to get ready for winter weather in their part of the country. Have them tell, dramatize, or draw a picture to show some part of the preparation.

Use the fruits and vegetables "harvested" in the fall and let children suggest how they could be used to make parts of a Thanksgiving dinner or another meal. Ask children to make up recipes for the "dishes" they dream up. If it is near Thanksgiving, ask them to show which foods they are most thankful for. Have them decide what would be served if the "first Thanksgiving" was being celebrated this year.

On Columbus Day, let children pretend to be Columbus sailing on a long voyage. Explain some of the concerns that his sailors had about sailing across an ocean they knew nothing about. Use a flat piece of paper and a globe to demonstrate any necessary concepts. Have them show what might have happened if the earth had been flat by using sheets of papers and "little" ships.

Ask children to make up a story about the adventures of two pumpkins as they go from a patch in a cornfield, to a farmer's market, and then to a child's house to become Halloween jack-o'-lanterns. Tell them that the pumpkins can talk. Have them make up the conversation between the two pumpkins.

# A STORY FOR FALL

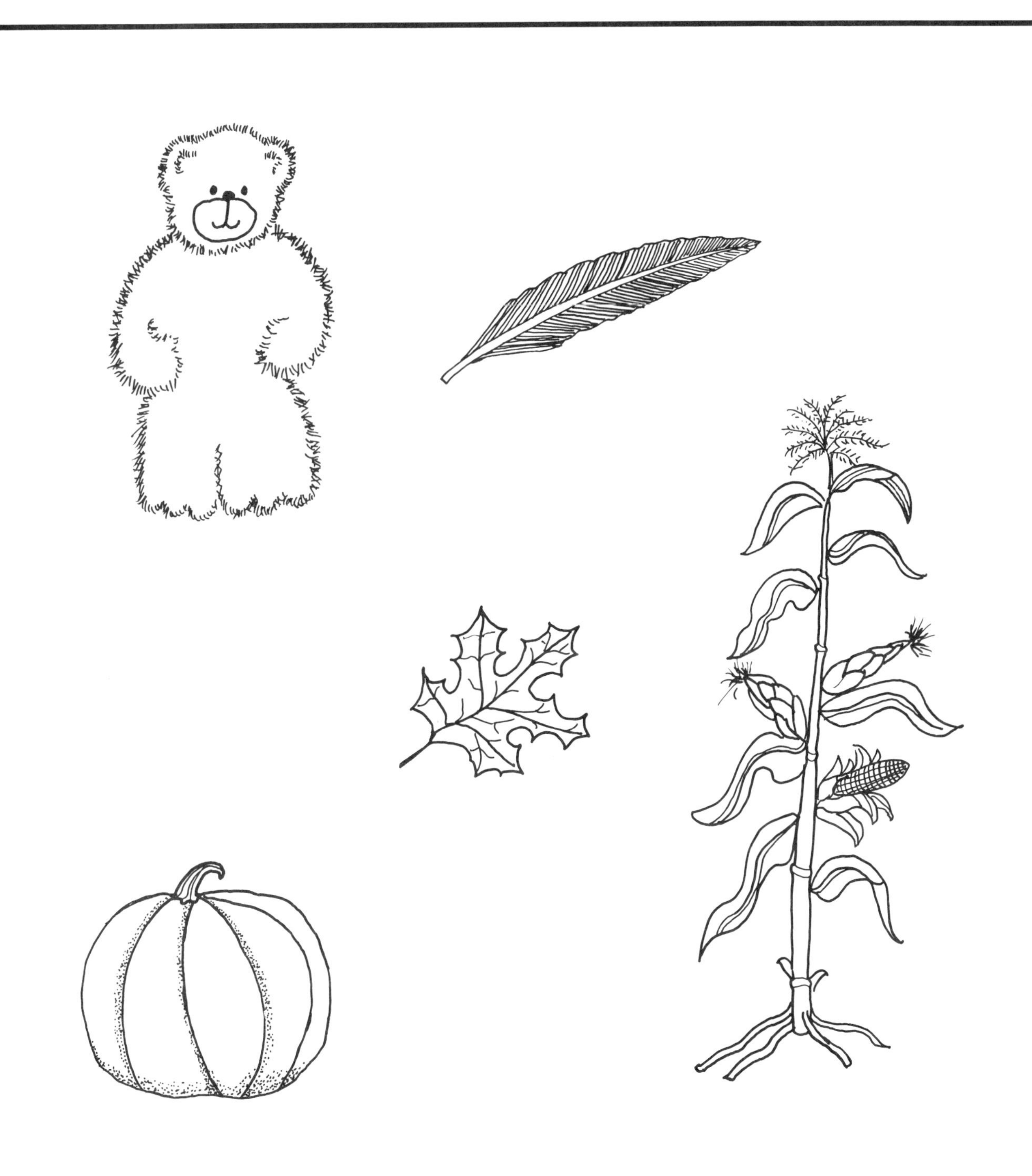

Children can tell or write a story about fall, using these objects as story starters.
(bear, feather, leaf, pumpkin, corn)

# WINTER

**Detail**
*What's Your Winter Like Now?*

To understand what season of the year is taking place, it is important to be able to describe what the weather is like. There are lots of details to consider. Since, in many places a number of different varieties of weather occur during the winter, this is a good time to talk in more depth about the weather.

Make a special type of calendar in which there is room in each box by the number to place a picture of what the weather is like that day. Ask children to help you make symbols for each type of weather condition possible in their location. These might include the following: mitten (cold), white blob or cotton (cloudy), gray blob (fog), snowperson or snowflake (snowy), umbrella (rainy), yellow circle (sunny), ice cube (freezing), fan (hot). Each day, have children use different words to describe the temperature, the cloud conditions, and the appearance of the sky. Then, have them decide which symbol goes in the box.

**Comparison**
*Is Everything the Same?*

An important part of weather prediction is making comparisons about weather that has occurred before and whether similar conditions will happen again. Children can use the weather calendar and their own memories as they discuss likenesses and differences. Several winter details lend themselves to making comparisions.

Help children become more familiar with temperature concepts by assisting them to do the HOT-COLD HANDS experiments. Ask them to also think about how the different temperatures affect the types of clothing that they wear. Have children decide what temperature word should be given to a day. Then, have them draw or cut out pictures to show what special clothing is needed for that temperature.

Point out the fact that scientists believe that each snowflake that falls has its own design. Pass out sheets of white paper and scissors. Show children how to fold each sheet two or three times. Demonstrate then how they are to cut out different shapes on each of the folds. Let them make their own snowflakes and then compare the details in theirs with those made by other children. You may want to hang them on the branches of a real or pretend tree.

**Classification**
*Tell Us About Winter*

As children talk about different types of weather, they are gathering knowledge about the category "winter." In places where the weather does not change that much during the year, children will need to learn other indicators, too.

Ask children to name or find pictures that show weather or special events that occur most often in the winter. These may include snowfalls, cold weather, certain holiday celebrations, children whose birthdays occur between December and April, or happenings that are specific to their area. Use any pictures found to make a Winter Bulletin Board. You may need to describe what winter is like in other places. Children may also want to describe what fall had been like and make comparisons between the two seasons.

# HOT-COLD HANDS

**YOU'LL NEED:**

3 bowls

tap water:
- very warm
- tepid
- cold

**WHAT TO DO:**

1. Set out 3 bowls. Fill one side bowl with very warm water. Fill the other side bowl with cold water.

2. Fill the middle bowl with tepid or room temperature water.

3. Child places one hand into the very warm water bowl and the other hand into the cold water bowl, at the same time.

4. Identify the sensations.

5. Child then plunges both hands into the middle bowl. Ask child what he feels.☆

6.

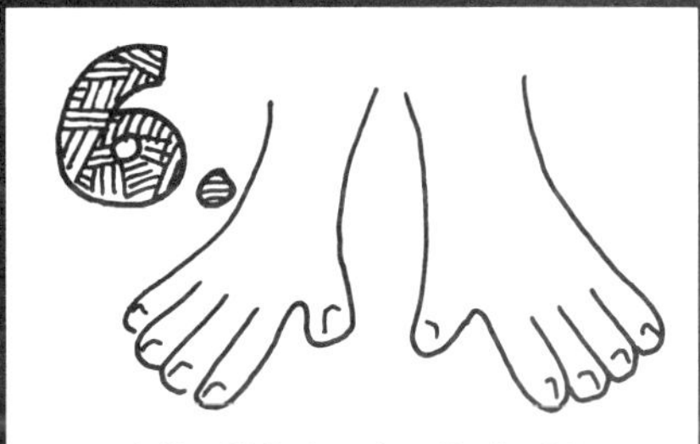

☆ THE HAND THAT WAS COLD WILL FEEL WARM AND THE HAND THAT WAS WARM WILL FEEL COLD

# WINTER

**Sequence**

*What Has Already Happened?*

Weather forecasting has people thinking about what is going to happen next. The "forecasters" make their choice by studying the sequence of what has happened in other places. Your room calendar with its record of earlier weather can be used when talking about what has taken place.

Help children record the different kinds of weather on some type of calendar. Ask them to talk about the weather that occurred during the month. Encourage them to use words such as "before," "after," "next day," "last week," and "this month."

**Cause and Effect**

*Why Does This Happen?*

The study of weather and why the different types of it occur when they do is very fascinating. Do some experiments to demonstrate some of the causes of weather conditions.

Make it possible for children to see a teakettle that has water boiling in it and steam coming out of its spout. Hold a glass filled with ice cubes so that the steam reaches the bottom of the glass. Ask children to tell what occurs—water drops like rain—and why they think it happened.

Do experiments, such as the ones suggested in FREEZING FUN, so that children can see what happens when water is placed where the temperatures are below the freezing level. You may want to let children keep track of how long it takes to freeze the water solid enough to make the ice blocks.

**Inference**

*What Do You Think Takes Place?*

Children need lots of experience with the step-by-step development of each type of weather or with using the results of any special type of weather. Letting children explain how they make something will help them fill in the gaps.

With real snow, ice blocks made as a part of FREEZING FUN, or other materials that can be molded, have children describe the steps they would follow if they were to make a snowperson or a snowhouse. Keep track of the directions as they are given. Help children choose what they are going to make and aid them in following the steps in order. When necessary, ask for additional directions.

**Predicting Outcomes**

*What Should I Wear?*

Children are probably already aware that many people listen to weather reports so they can make decisions about what they will wear or do on the following day or week. They should be made aware of the clues that help people make choices. In addition, they should have practice indicating the effect of making a certain prediction.

Use the calendar on which you and the children have been recording the different types of weather as the basis of discussions. One day, talk about the different kinds of activities that people can do when a certain weather condition takes place. Have children predict what would be the best kinds of clothing to wear. At another time, pick a different type of weather and describe how the children will be dressed. As them to predict what activities would be the most fun to do in that weather.

# FREEZING FUN

**YOU'LL NEED:**

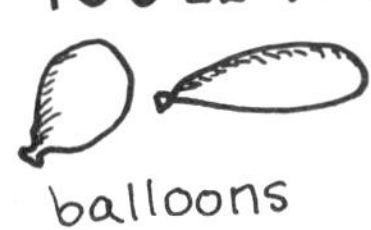

- balloons
- rubber or plastic gloves
- elastic bands
- real flowers
- ice cube tray
- fruits: strawberries, grapes, blue berries, cherries, orange
- paper milk containers

**WHAT TO DO:**

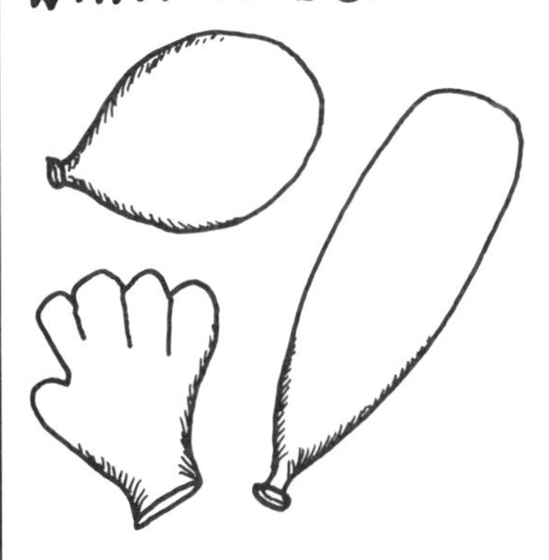

## ICE SHAPES

Adult, with children, fills balloons and plastic glove with water. Secure tightly with elastic bands. Place outside in freezing temperatures or in the freezer.

Leave for 24 hours.

Remove from freezer, or bring indoors, and tear away plastic or rubber.

Use as decorations or float in tub of water as ice bergs.

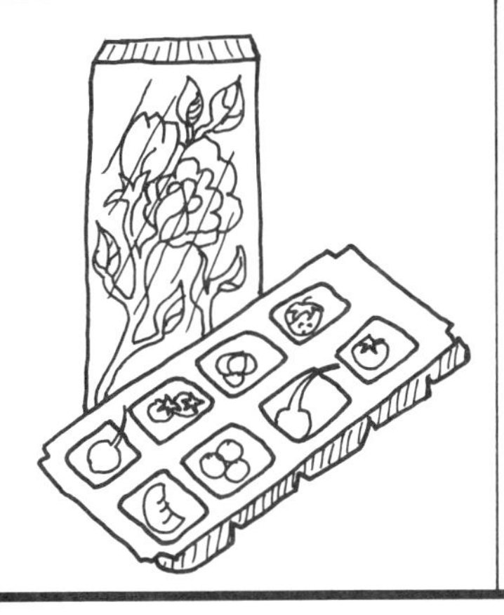

## FANCY ICE CUBES

Place one piece of fruit into each section of an ice cube tray. Place flowers in quart or half gallon paper milk containers. Adult or children pour previously boiled and totally cooled water into both containers almost to the top. Freeze out of doors or in freezer.

Use cubes in cold drinks.

Tear away milk carton paper and use block of ice and flowers as a centerpiece.

## ICE BLOCKS

Fil various sized paper milk containers with water. Set outside in freezing temperatures. Leave overnight.

Tear away paper containers and assemble frozen ice blocks into a fort or other building.

# CREATIVE THINKING

Read or tell the story *The Mystery of the Missing Red Mitten* by Stephen Kellogg. Explain that a little girl has lost one of her mittens and she is trying to remember where she left it. Tell them that the little girl wonders if some mice might be using the lost mitten as a sleeping bag or if a mother bird is using the mitten as a cap for a baby bird. Then, ask children to use their imagination as they think about the mitten and answer some of the following questions.

- "What other things can you do with a mitten in the winter besides wearing it?"
- "If you had lost a red mitten in winter, where would you look for it?"
- "In the story, the girl wonders what would grow if the red mitten was planted? What do you think?"

Have children describe different types of winter days—cold, snowy, blowy, raining, sunshiny, foggy. Let them each pick a kind of day mentioned. Ask some of the questions that follow.

- "What can you do on your special day when you go outside?"
- "What might you do, if you have to stay inside?"
- "What clothes or equipment do you need to wear or have wherever you are going to play?"

Let children pretend that a big snowstorm has taken place. Have them decide what will happen in homes, schools, stores, and other places with which they are familiar. Ask children to show, with their hands or some blocks, varying depths of the snow. Have them demonstrate how they would walk through these depths. Let them tell what types of foot coverings would be the best and which ones would not work.

Provide each child with a paper cup containing an ice cube. Let each one think about placing his cup where the ice cube will last the longest amount of time. Encourage each child to find a different place and then to tell what the place is like. Encourage children to include in their descriptions whether the place is in a dark spot, how cool it is, if the cup will be inside something else, and any other important observations. Ask children to help you decide how often the cubes should be checked. Set a timer for the period of time suggested. After all the cubes have melted, help children decide which was the best place.

Have children think about how to do outside activities inside or the inside ones outdoors. You might begin by asking them to think about making a snowperson inside a home or classroom. Have them consider all the equipment or points that are needed or must be remembered.

# THIS IS ME...

Child draws a picture of self dressed in winter clothing appropriate for your area.

# SPRING

**Detail**
*Spring Scavenger Hunt*

There are so many things that children can hunt for as they go for walks. Since the signs of spring do not start appearing at the same time, this activity can cover a number of weeks.

First, be sure the children can name the flower, bird, leaf, or whatever is being hunted. Use pictures such as the ones on page 52 to let them know what things they are looking for. Ask them to describe each by its shape, color, or size. Depending upon your part of the country, children may be able to look for some of the following "signs" of spring: spring blossoms—forsythia, pussywillow, cherry, apple; birds—robins, swallows, nest building; spring flowers—crocuses, tulips; snow melting; dandelion plants; bugs. After each hunt, let them show or talk about the object or events they found with a picture or verbal description.

Let children make imaginary bugs as suggested in BUGS, BUGS, BUGS. . . Have them tell you what details they are going to include as they make their bugs.

**Detail/Comparison**
*Color Chart*

Make a class color chart or individual ones for each child. Write each color name and have children make a sample of the color below each name.

Let children make one tally mark for each color they see as they take a walk. Point out that if they see a red cardinal and a red tulip, they can make two marks. If some children want to make a green mark and a red mark for a red tulip on a green stem, encourage this. Take this type of walk several different times so children can compare the color changes as a plant, such as forsythia, develops. Have them compare the colors of different flowers.

**Classification**
*Where Does It Fit?*

Children like to pick up all different types of items as they are walking. Let them carry brown bags or plastic milk cartons for their collections.

Later, help children group the earlier chosen objects in different categories that you or they may suggest. Below are some of the groups that might be included: types of materials, size, color, texture, living and nonliving.

**Sequence**
*How Did It Grow?*

Children need to "see" the time passage involved in the growth of plants.

Help each child find a new plant, such as a dandelion or a tulip. Have the group insert tongue depressors next to their plants. Show them how to mark how high each plant is. Write the date next to each mark. Help them watch the plant each day. Depending upon how fast the plant grows, choose another day on which they are to mark how high theirs are at that point. Continue the process until each plant is fully grown. You may wish to mark your calendar also with the dates.

# Bugs, Bugs, Bugs...

YOU'LL NEED:

plasticene clay

glue

natural items

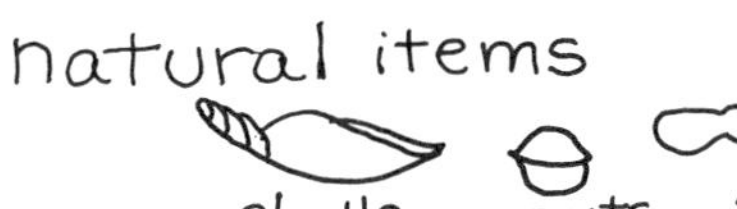

shells nuts

seeds

twigs leaves

cardboard 5"x8"

WHAT TO DO:

1. Assemble natural items on cardboard to resemble an imaginary bug.

2. Glue each part down onto cardboard.

or...

3. Using clay as a base, attach natural items to it to make 3-dimensional model bugs.

# SPRING

**Cause and Effect**
*What Happens When It Rains?*

In nature, many events bring about certain results. Springtime, when so many changes in nature take place, is a good season in which to discuss both effects and their causes.

Take children on a walk during a gentle spring rain if all the children have rain gear or, if not, just after that rain. Here are some suggested activities. Do them and discuss the effect that occurred. Then, have the children tell what caused that result.

- Have children stand under a low-boughed tree. Shake one of the branches.
- Provide children with the opportunity to watch puddles form. Have them talk about why puddles form and why in only certain places.
- Have children place twigs in water moving down the sides of a street. Ask questions such as "Why is it moving along?" and "Where will the twig (or water) go?" Have them place a rock in the middle of a stream and then talk about the effect of damming up the stream.
- Place objects that you have brought along such as paper, feathers, chalk, plastic, cotton fabric, and a slice of bread somewhere the falling rain can hit them for a few minutes. Ask children to tell what happened to each item and why.

**Inference**
*What Happens and Why?*

Children take many events for granted without filling in the missing steps. Do some experiments with balloons step by step on a breezy day so they can fill in or figure out the gaps.

Talk about the steps in getting balloons ready to fly. Let the air out of a balloon and then blow it up again. Provide each child with a blown-up balloon on a string. Take children for a walk so they can see how a gentle breeze or still air affects the balloons. Then, discuss what is keeping the balloons up or what is making them bob up and down. Take children back to the room and have them note what happens. Discuss why the balloons are not floating high up.

Help children prepare the GRASSY EGGHEADS. Have them discuss each step. Then, have them watch to see in which egghead the grass grows first. Help them discuss why this occurred.

**Predicting Outcomes**
*What Do You Think Will Happen?*

Because so many events "start" in the spring, children can guess how the situations are going to continue. Some outcomes are easy because the same thing happens every year—birds build nests, tulips grow from bulbs; however, others just depend upon the day.

On a day when it suddenly clouds up, ask children what they think is going to happen. Have them decide what they might do or what they might wear according to whether they predicted it might rain or that it might get colder. Another day, reverse the process and show them some rainy day clothes or mittens and ask them to predict the type of weather.

# GRASSY EGGHEADS

**YOU'LL NEED:**

5 cardboard strips (6" x ½")

5 empty eggshell halves
plastic wrap
sponge
cotton puff
coffee grounds
vermiculite
soil
grass seed
glue
water mister
marker

**WHAT TO DO:**

Adult makes a cardboard collar to set the eggshell into by gluing the ends of the cardboard strip together. Place eggshell on collar.

Fill each eggshell half with one of the following:
- a sponge
- a cotton puff
- soil
- vermiculite
- coffee grounds

Sprinkle one teaspoon grass seed over materials in each egg.

Dampen seeds in each eggshell with water mister. Cover egg halves with plastic wrap.

For one week: keep seeds moist and out of direct sunlight.
After one week: uncover seed sprouts and place in direct sunlight

Use marker to draw faces on eggshells.

# CREATIVE THINKING

Let children watch how birds build nests and notice what happens after the nest is completed. Because the growth cycle of the bird occurs so quickly, children can see the development from the nest to the egg stage to the bird learning to fly. Picture cards can be made of each event as it takes place. Then, children can arrange them in the proper sequence. These same types of cards also can be made with plant development, the steps involved in planning and implementing a garden, or the stages in the life of a butterfly.

Have children gather the same types of materials that a bird does—straw, grass, twigs, yarn, string. Let them experiment with trying to "build" a nest. You may wish to let them make two-dimensional nests by fastening the materials onto sheets of cardboard.

Have children make paper bag or sock puppets of their favorite flowers. Then, let them (or "the puppet") give information about themselves, including their names, what colors they are, where they like to grow, and what they think will happen to them—be picked, eaten, die when it gets cold.

Help children find a tree or bush to "adopt." Provide time for them to observe it daily. Have them lie on their backs and think about the tree and what is special about the place where it grows. Ask them to speculate about that living object—has someone or something lived in it, what changes have occurred to it, and so on.

Help children make individual books to record things about spring they like: colorful items, things with shapes they like, things that make them feel good. If children want to "write" in their books, help them with names, colors, or short sentences or stories.

Have children take a walk and talk about the new growth appearing. Ask them to decide what is not changing and might be considered "old." Point out that a tree or bush are old, but that old items can grow new parts.

Encourage children to collect the sounds of spring. Have a tape recorder handy so that children can tell you when to record. Later on, play the tape back and have them tell what they think might make sounds like that. Encourage them to imagine other "noisemakers" besides the actual object that might make the same sounds.

Have children walk fast for several minutes outside on a sunny day. Point to the shade under a tree. Ask them to predict how they will feel if they sit under the shade of that tree. Then, let them find out if their predictions were true.

# SPRING SCAVENGER HUNT

Try to find these things while outside on a walk. Color each picture.

# SUMMER

**Detail**

*What Is It?*

Children have been in school for a while and have met a lot of items in their nature walks, so it's time to see what details they remember. Make a game out of identifying some of the objects they have seen and talked about as they take walks during the summer. Use items that have distinctive characteristics, such as leaves, pine cones, succulents, bark, rocks, and flowers.

Place some of the objects picked up on one or more of the walks in a paper bag. As you do so, have children name each one. Have a child hold onto one of the objects inside the bag. Ask her to talk about how it feels. Let the other children guess what is being described.

If you have a beach nearby, take children there to pick up shells. Then, have the group sit in a shady spot. Spread the shells out. Ask a child to describe a shell without pointing to it. Have others pick out that shell and point out other details. Let children decide which shells they want to use while making their POSTER WORD design.

**Comparison/Classification**

*Float or Sink*

Provide a bowl full of objects that will sink and float. You might use objects such as the following: buttons, coins, nails, rocks, corks, pieces of styrofoam, balloon, and spools. Set out a low, plastic bowl with water in it and some kitchen tongs. Let children use the tongs to pick up an object and gently place it in the bowl and see what happens. Then, have them sort the objects into those that float and those that sink. Allow time for them to feel each object and to decide why it floated or sank.

**Sequence**

*How Hot Is It? How Cool Is It?*

Children should be made aware of the differences in meaning of words that describe and that go from one extreme to the other. Adults use words such as warm, hot, sweltering, tepid, lukewarm or cold, crisp, cool, nippy, chilly, shivering, freezing, without letting children know the differences or showing them the order in which they occur.

Help children experience the differences in temperatures. As the summer progresses and the temperature changes, help them use different adjectives to describe how they or the weather feels. Write down the temperature at a certain time each day. Beside the number, write the word you and the children decide describes the day. You also might want to note some special activity that occurred that day. At the end of a week or two, help children arrange the words so that they go from one extreme to the other.

# POSTER WORD

**YOU'LL NEED:**

poster or illustration board (18"X24")

pencil

glue

brush

clear acrylic spray

rocks shells sand

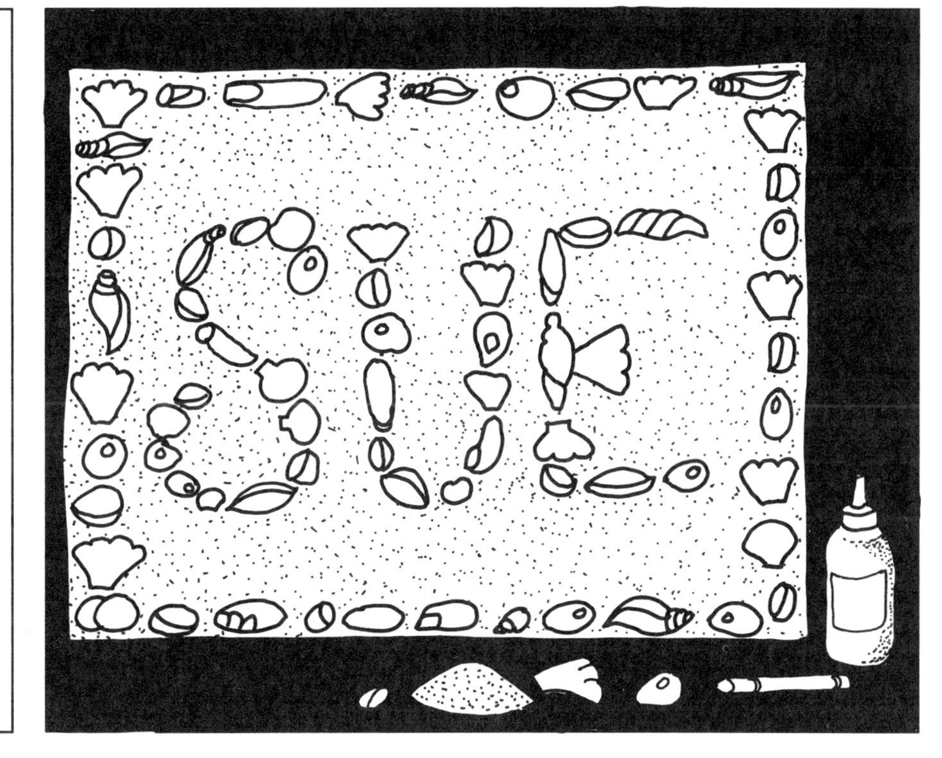

**WHAT TO DO:**

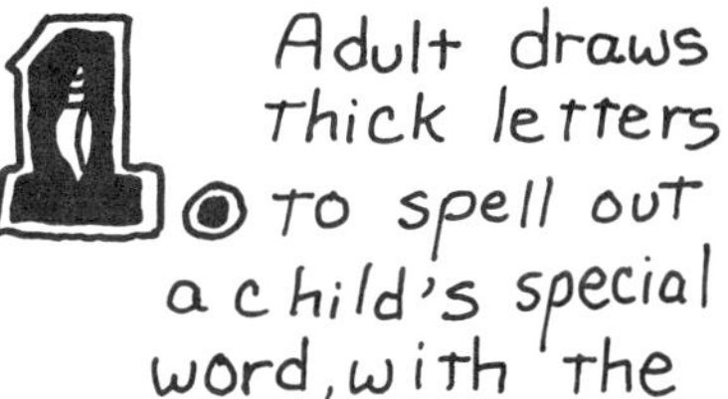

1. Adult draws thick letters to spell out a child's special word, with the pencil, on posterboard.

2. Have children apply glue, with a brush, over the pencilled letters and place shells on glue.

3. Use rocks and shells to frame the edges of the posterboard.

4. Appy a thin wash of glue, with a brush, over uncovered areas and sprinkle sand over all.

5. Let dry overnight. Hold poster, tilt slightly, and give it a shake to remove excess sand.

6. Spray with clear acrylic to seal poster. (Use acrylic spray in a well-ventilated area.)

# SUMMER

**Cause and Effect**
*Just Add Water*

Adding water in certain situations can cause different effects. Let children do lots of experiments on their own. Present some planned activities, too. Children then can see what happens each time.

Below are several different experiments. Provide the materials and let children do "their own thing." Talk about the effects as they occur.

- Have dry sponges. Let children add water and see how the sponges grow in size and become softer.
- Provide a jar with a lid, paper towels, seeds, and water. Have a child wet the towels and place them in the jar. Ask another child to put seeds on the damp towels and close the jar. Wait a few days.
- Provide some white sugar and let children taste a grain or two. Let children add water and stir. Suggest that they may want to taste a small sip of the water. Let them talk about what happened to the sugar.
- Provide a dish of cornstarch. Have children add a few drops of water at a time until the mixture is like dough. Let children pick up the mixture and see how it crumbles.
- Provide the materials suggested in SAND STORYTELLERS. Let children see what they can do after the sand has been moistened. (As children make up stories, many cause and effect situations will develop.)

**Inference**
*What Do You Know About?*

In order for children to make inferences, they have to have the background of knowledge in order to "guess" about a situation. Before children do experiments on their own, assess their knowledge of water by asking some questions.

Bring children close enough to a basin of water so they can see it. Ask each child to touch the water. Suggested points you may bring up or that you may need to give additional experiences with are included in parentheses.

- "What things do you know about water?" (it's wet; it moves around; it makes noise when you splash it; you can see your reflection in it)
- "What do you like about water?" (you can shower or swim in it; it tastes good when you are thirsty; it helps you make mud pies)
- "What can you do with water?" (drink it; wash with it; cook things in it; brush teeth after wetting brush; swim in it; mix other things into it)

**Predicting Outcomes**
*Playing "Change"*

Using the knowledge gained from the experiments above, let children predict what will happen in the following situations.

- Pretend that a boy and girl have been playing outside in the mud and their hands have become quite dirty.
- Pretend that the children's clothes have become quite dirty because they have been sliding around on the ground.
- Pretend that the children's clean clothes are hanging on a clothesline and it begins to rain.
- Pretend that very dark clouds have come along when a girl with an umbrella and a boy without an umbrella go for a walk.

# SAND STORYTELLERS

**YOU'LL NEED:**

sand 

water

blocks 

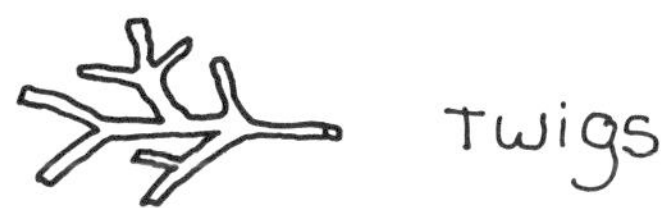 twigs

 rocks

 shells

**WHAT TO DO:**

1. Pour water into sand until moistened. Use a block drawn across the sand to make roads.

2. Rocks, shells, twigs can become buildings, parks and ponds.

3. Use markers to draw faces on rocks to create people. Children make up stories.

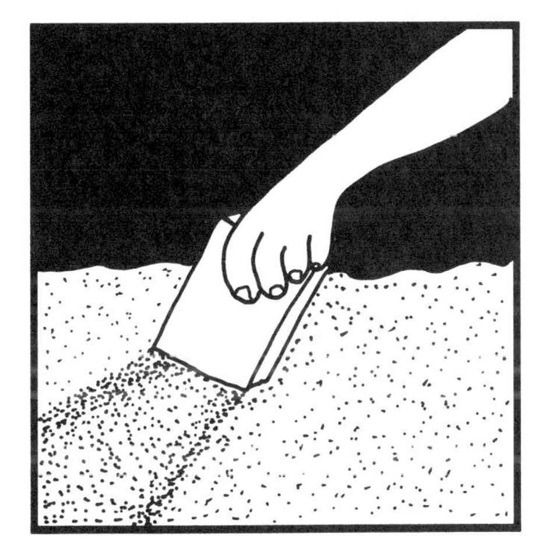

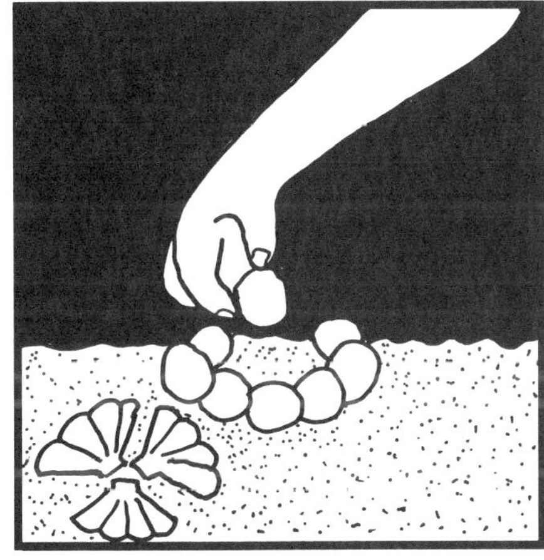

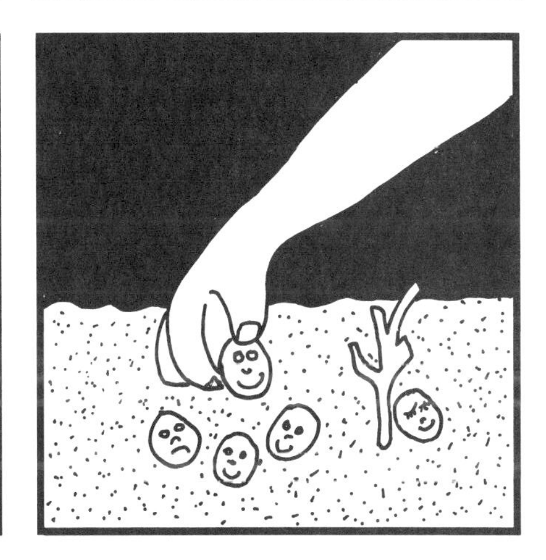

# A SEASONAL SCENE

Have children choose a season of the year and illustrate that season in this country scene. They may use drawings, or cut and paste magazine pictures or glue photos onto these pages. Children can show people doing seasonal activities such as swimming in the pond or ice skating in

winter. The trees can have green summer leaves, colorful fall leaves, spring blossoms or no leaves at all. Have children explain what happens in the season they chose. Ask them to guess what the temperature might be.

Mud, sand, flour, and clay allow children to give "shape" to their imaginations. One game they enjoy is for each child to make a "creature" out of any of the materials. Let the children add water when necessary. Have the child name what it is or let another child guess what has been made. Have a child pose a "problem situation" that one of their creatures has gotten into and let the others develop solutions for "saving the day."

Let children pour water or sand from one container to another of a different size or shape. Ask them to find other unusual containers. Allow them to experiment more with water, sand, and containers.

Place wet sand on an edged cookie sheet. Let children make different types of footprints in it, using their own feet and those of a doll or toy animal.

Have children figure out how to make their own mud. Encourage them to construct roads, mountains, houses, fences, animals, and so on with their own hands and mud. You also may wish to have plastic containers or scraps nearby that they can use.

Summertime often means a brown bag picnic. Those paper bags can be used for other activities, too. Play such games as "Rock, Rock, Who Has the Rock?" While children are eating, place a small rock in one of the sacks. Tell them that whoever has the rock should try to put it in someone else's bag without being seen. Have this continue until lunch is over. Ask children to try to figure out who has the rock. Then, have each child pick out a crayon. When they are through with their lunch sacks, have them tear the sacks open. Let them use the sack and the crayon to make rubbings of something they find outside, such as bark, sidewalks, fences, stone, or brick walls.

Language develops through the eyes. Let children describe such summer experiences as the following:

- a rainbow after a summer shower
- a kitten playing in the tall grass
- the tiny world of ants
- a ladybug crawling up a flower stem
- the sound of water flowing over pebbles

Help children place a few drops of red, blue, and yellow paint on a paper plate on a rainy day. Let them set the plate in the rain for a few minutes and see what happens. Have them note the design and colors that form and then use the new colors in a painting.

Let children think about what their favorite summer activities are. Have them take turns acting out situations. Let the others guess which activity is being portrayed.

# LANGUAGE DEVELOPMENT

# LANGUAGE DEVELOPMENT

**Detail/Comparison**
*Feely Box*

Many children learn about their environments primarily through touch. Others enjoy using the kinesthetic approach to give added depth to what they already know. Having the opportunity to actually experience what certain words in their language mean enables children to better understand those words. Prepare a "feely" box by cutting two holes in a large-size container. Each hole should be about 6" x 6". Glue a square of scrap fabric like a flap over one hole so the contents of the box can be hidden from view and so new objects can be added.

Provide opportunities for some of the following activities so that children can discuss the experiences using appropriate adjectives.

- Place different classroom items inside. Have children place one hand in the box, tell what an item feels like, and then identify it by name.
- Place items of different textures in the box—cotton ball, sandpaper, jacks, corrugated cardboard—and let children describe an item or pick out the one that fits a certain description.
- Place three items—two the same and one that is different—inside the box. Ask children to describe the feel of each item and to name it. Have them tell which one is different.

**Classification**
*What Belongs Together?*

When children are trying to develop an understanding of items that can be categorized as a member of a certain group, seeing the actual objects or pictures of them helps a great deal. They are better able to see specific details and grasp the similarities between the members of the group. Preparing a PICTURE WORD BOOK about a certain category provides the children with an excellent opportunity to classify pictures.

Help children decide what category of word "pictures" each will collect—cars, food, people, and so on. Have them talk about some of the similar details in items that can belong in the group that they chose. Let them find pictures and make pages for their books. You may wish to label pictures for those children who want to "read" names. Cut out your own pictures that will fit in the categories that the children have specified. Hold up each cutout and have the child whose category it belongs to identify the picture and add it to the last page in the book.

**Sequence**
*First, Next, Last*

Place three books that have distinctive covers on a table in a left-to-right order. Point to each book and have it described. Find out if children know the meaning of the words "first," "next," and "last." If not, introduce the concepts by pointing to each book and naming its position. Then, place three other items somewhere and have children tell what object is in each position.

As children do a usual classroom routine, such as drawing a picture, ask them questions that include the words "before" and "after."

- "After you choose a red crayon, what do you draw?"
- "Before you cut out a snowflake, what do you need to do?"
- "After you finish your juice, what do you do next?"

# PICTURE WORD BOOK

YOU'LL NEED:

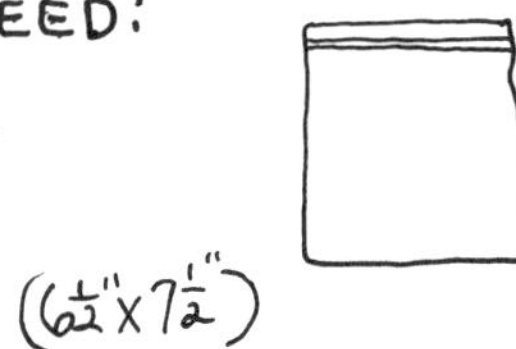

- 5 posterboard pieces ($6\frac{1}{2}$" x $7\frac{1}{2}$")
- 6 plastic locking bags
- paperclips
- glue
- button/carpet thread
- cut out magazine pictures
- needle

WHAT TO DO:

1. (Adult makes book) Cut out and glue pictures to both sides of posterboard pieces.

2. Place each posterboard "page" into a baggie so ziplocking section is on the left side.

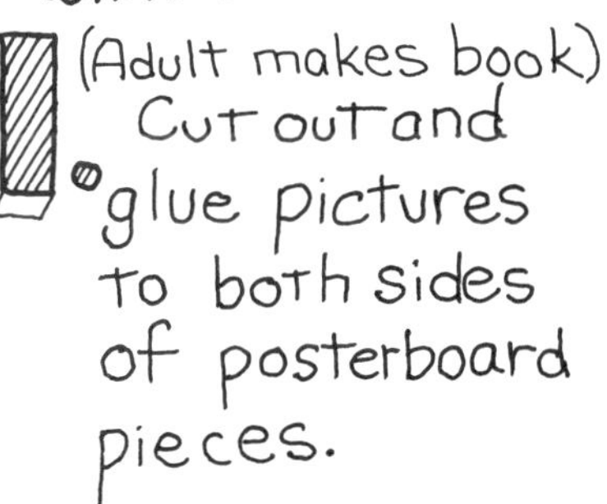

3. Place all 5 poster board and bag 'pages' together with ziplocking sections on left.

4. Add one more ziplocking bag, but place this last page with the open section <u>on top</u>. Leave bag empty.

5. Use paper clips to hold all 6 bags tightly together so all edges line up.

6. Use the needle and thread to sew through all layers of plastic, down the left side. Knot the end.

# LANGUAGE DEVELOPMENT

**Cause and Effect**
*Add the Words*

Wordless books develop the imagination and vocabulary as children tell a story as they "see it." Each event in the story will lead to an ensuing result, so children can talk about a lot of causes and their effects.

Books, such as *Skates* by Ezra Jack Keats, in which two dogs experiment with their newly found roller skates and get entangled with a kitten family, provide many opportunities for children to talk about the effects of what the dogs and kittens do. As you enter into any discussions of the stories, use conjunctions such as "because," "so," or "since" if children do not include them. Encourage them to figure out why each event occurs.

Let children make their own books, using the directions for the WHAT HAPPENS WHEN books. Encourage them to make pictures for their own stories that show a cause on one page—rain coming down, for instance—and an effect of that event on the next page—a child with an umbrella, boots, and a raincoat or one playing in some big puddles.

**Cause and Effect**
*Hide and Seek*

Take a comic strip or sections of a picture book and place them around the room. Give a child the first picture and let him describe it and decide what comes next and tell why. Have children hunt around the room to find the picture they think comes next. Let them compare their "effect" with the one pictured.

**Inference**
*Mystery Picture*

Children need lots of practice in making guesses. They need to use their eyes and background knowledge to discover clues that will help them guess the correct or most possible answers.

Mount a number of good-sized pictures on sheets of cardboard. Put each in a large envelope. Have children pull out one of the pictures slightly and tell what they think they are seeing. Ask them to guess what the picture might be from seeing just the little part showing and to tell why they think so. Allow as many children to guess as possible. Suggest that children take more of a peek, talk about any additional clues they see, and decide if their first guesses were right. You also may want to place a mask over the picture that has only a small hole in the center. Let children decide from the very small clues what the big picture is about. Listen to the choices given.

**Predicting Outcomes**
*Acting It Out*

Children are better able to understand picture stories when they can put themselves in similar situations and act out what is taking place. Then, they can fill in gaps and figure out more easily what the outcome of the situation may be.

Find a picture, photo, or drawing of a scene in which a number of children are included. Note what props are included in the picture and provide similar ones. Have children imitate the picture by placing the props where they belong, make up some conversation, and decide what will happen next in the situation. Ask them to act out the next part of the story in words and deeds. Discuss how the props will be moved as the next part of the story takes place.

# WHAT HAPPENS WHEN...

**YOU'LL NEED:**

- a long piece of sturdy paper
- markers
- crayons

**WHAT TO DO:**

1. Cut or piece together a long length of paper. It should be 24" long and 6" tall.

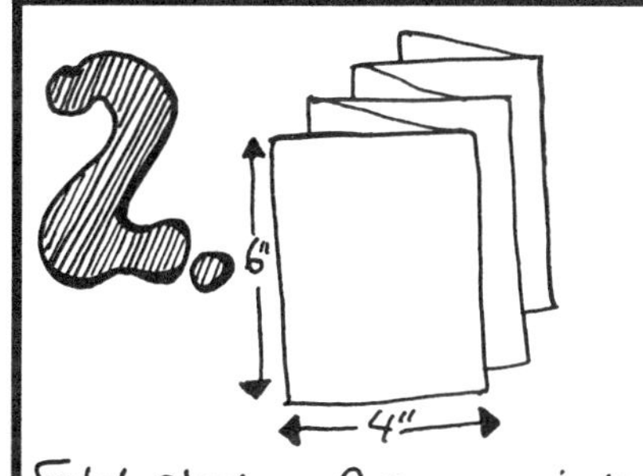


2. Fold strip of paper into 6 parts. Each 'page' is 6" tall and 4" wide.

3. On the first page (cover) have children draw a form of weather and adult can title it. (see samples)

4. Have children open up pages of the book and draw in things that go with that weather condition. You label.

5. Refold the book and have child "read his story". Discuss different ways we react to various weather conditions.

# words alive

Bring words to life by having children demonstrate their meanings in a real, active way. Using a chair as the only prop, children can show the meanings of the little prepositional words: on, over, around, under at, in, out. Another child or adult calls out one word, such as "around". Children respond by acting out that word. "Around" can mean "walk around" the chair, or "surround" the chair with one's arms. Let children use their own interpretations. Each is correct if the child 'solves the problem'. Encourage children to observe other solutions.

Now have children expand their ways of interpreting these words. Again, call out a word, such as "under." Children can use anything in class to show the meaning of that word. They might crawl under a table, or place a toy under a pillow.

After a while, move from this active interpretation of prepositional words into more abstract ways by using the "Where is my Little Dog Going?" page. Children can create a story using one or two doghouses and their dogs. They can think about these discussion questions:

"If a bigger dog came by, where would your dog go?"
"If there was a flood, where would the dog go?"
"If a cat family took over the doghouse, what would happen?"

# Where Is My Little Dog Going?

Use this picture of a doghouse to reinforce directional words. Children draw a dog on a separate piece of paper. Children cut out dog pictures and respond to commands such as "place the dog on (or in, on top of, below, and so on) the house." Color the house and draw a background.

LANGUAGE DEVELOPMENT

# CREATIVE THINKING

Bring flowers, plants, and vegetables into the room. Let children make up conversations between two different growing things. Encourage them to think about each object and its special features. You might begin by introducing a cactus to a tall mother-in-law's tongue or have a carrot top ask a head of lettuce to a party.

Start out by presenting examples of nonsense compositions, such as "I'm going to ride my sandwich to school." Let children say and draw other examples.

Bring in different types and sizes of wood, rocks, or seeds. Let children talk about, compare, and classify the different types. Then, have them suggest different objects that can be made from or with the wood, rocks, or seeds. If children want to make bookends, people, paper weights, mosaics, jewelry, or flowers, provide them with any extra materials they need.

Play "Hide the Thimble" with children. Explain that each time they must hide the thimble or some other object in a different place and according to the word which you will give to them. Use the following words in turn as each finder has an opportunity to place the object somewhere in the room: "in," "outside of," "under," "behind," "in front of," "next to," "over," "below," "beneath," "on top of." As the rest of the group hides their eyes, direct the hider by saying "Put the thimble (in) something." After the object has been hidden in the proper type of place, have the hider say, "I have put the thimble (in) something." Let the group look for the thimble. Have the finder say, "I found the thimble (in) a ______________________."

Start a sentence, such as "I'm going to my grandmother's house and into my suitcase I will put my teddy bear." Ask children to start a similar sentence and suggest what they might want to take that would fit in a suitcase. For children who know their ABC's, you might ask them to suggest names of objects in alphabetical order. It can become a memory game if you ask children to remember the objects that the other children have already stated.

Have children seated on one side of the room and place an object on the other side. Ask children to name and to demonstrate different actions they can do with their feet in order to get to the object.

# MATH

# MATH

**Detail**
*It's the Name That Counts*

As children play, they encounter all types of math. Before children can do activities concerning mathematical concepts, they need to know the names of concepts and recognize amounts or shapes whenever these concepts occur. Help them with these names. Give them practice identifying what they see and telling how many there are. Have them help you develop the SCRAP COUNTING POSTER.

Have children help you make a "How Many?" box. Use a shoe box and cut a circular hole in one side just big enough for a small hand to fit through. On the other side, cut out a window and cover that space with clear plastic. Each day, let children put a differing amount of similar objects in the box. Encourage them to look through the window and count the objects without touching each first. Then, allow children to take the objects and count them. After a while, write each number as a child touches an object and says its number name.

**Comparison**
*One Here, One There*

Much of what children do in their play makes mathematical comparisons—how big, how fast, how heavy, how long. They also are comparing amounts when they show one-to-one correspondence.

At any snack or meal preparation time, have a child count the number of children present and then put out the right number of cups, napkins, plates, and any flatware needed. Have another child pass out the materials to individual children. Be sure to have the other children take their places so all can see that each one has been given the same items.

Provide several examples of a wide variety of pasta shapes. Hold up one kind and ask children to find all the pasta of that kind. Show them how to place an example of the kind they are looking for in front of them. Then, ask them compare each of the others until they find all the ones that are alike.

**Classification**
*Shapely Thinking*

Many mathematical activities include work with geometric shapes. Children should be given opportunities to classify these in various ways—going from simple types of categorization to more complex ones. Below are a series of directions to give children practice in sorting geometric objects.

- "Find another shape that is the same color as this one."
- "Point out all the blue shapes."
- "Sort all the objects into groups so each group shows a different shape.
- "Find all the shapes that are red."

**Sequence**
*The Order of Things*

In mathematics, order involves not only the sequential order of numbers, but also other patterns that exist. It helps to introduce the idea of numerical patterns by first having children extend patterns using geometric shapes.

Use six colored pattern or attribute blocks and make a pattern with them that children can copy right next to it. Then, let them extend that or another pattern by adding the additional shapes to the right of the pattern. In the beginning, the objects in the pattern should vary only in one attribute—color, shape, or size. Later, let them make up their own patterns.

# SCRAP COUNTING POSTER

**YOU'LL NEED:**

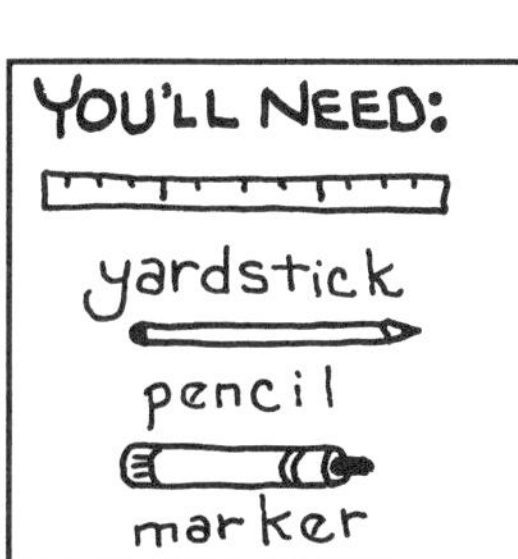


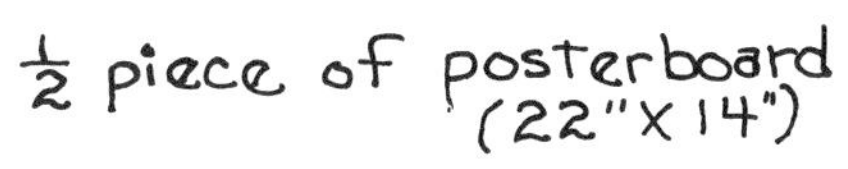

Scraps:
- styrofoam pieces
- caps
- coins
- corks
- shells

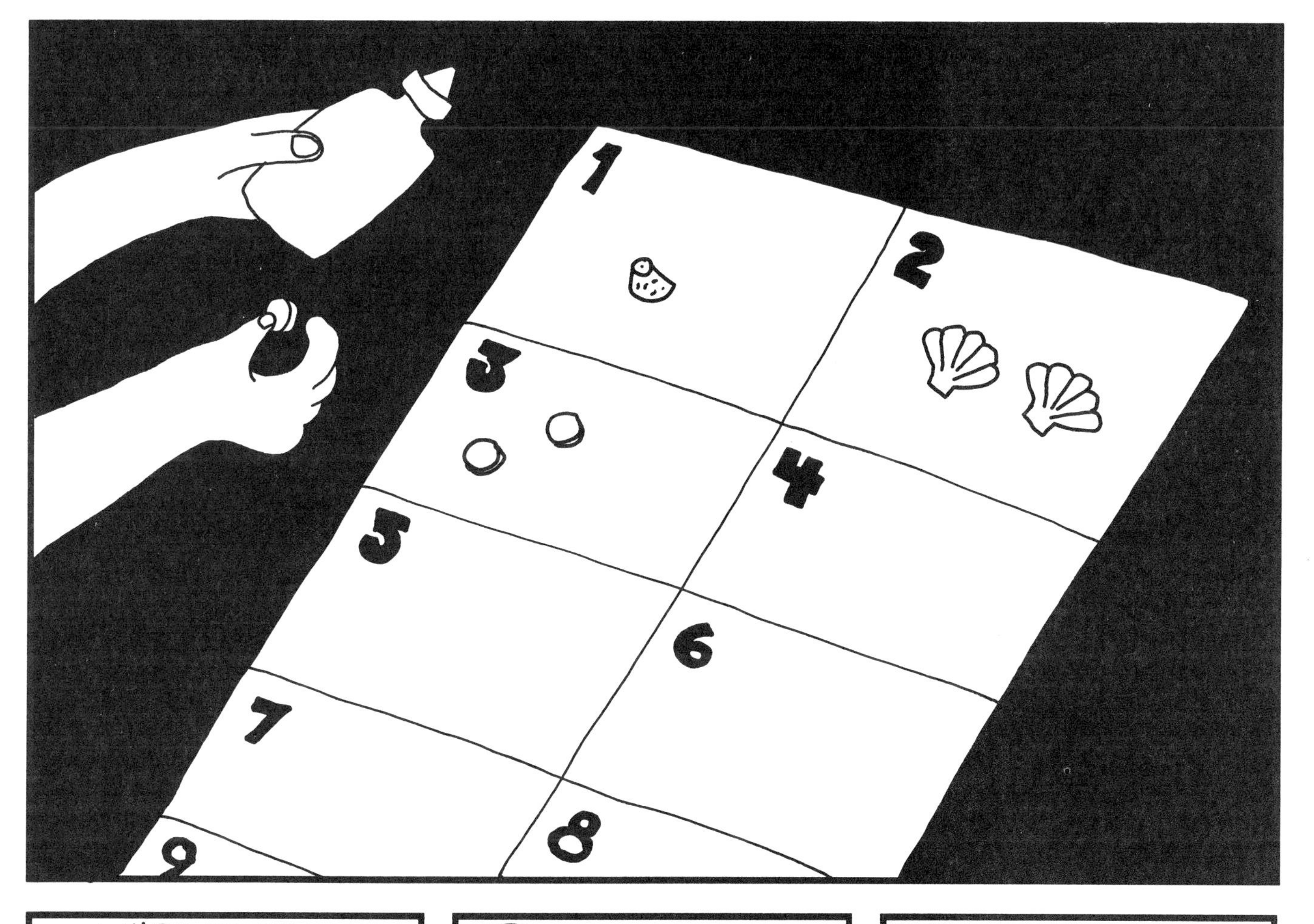


**WHAT TO DO:**

1. Adult premeasures and marks the piece of posterboard into 10 equal sections (each is approximately 4½" x 7")

2. Use marker to write in one number from 1-10 in each section.

3. Children glue on scrap items to correspond with number in each section. Encourage use of same items in each section.

# MATH

**Cause and Effect**
*More or Less?*

By allowing children to use real objects, it is possible for them to see the effect of adding, subtracting, multiplying, and dividing actual objects. When they actually move objects from one place to another and talk about what they are doing, children have an easier time understanding each mathematical process. Encourage them to use words like "because," "since," "so," "in order to," and "when."

Provide children with various types of macaroni—ziti, wagon wheels, elbows—and string or yarn. You may wish to use different food colors to add another attribute—color—to the patterns that children will develop as they string macaroni necklaces. Ask children to pick out two different shapes and to think of a pattern. Then, have them decide how many of each type they will need to make a necklace for themselves and pick those out. Ask them to count how many pieces of macaroni they chose. Then, provide time for children to make their necklaces. Children may see the need to add to or subtract macaroni from their necklaces. They also will see the effect of the continuous pattern they have created.

As children make SPICY COOKED APPLESAUCE discussed on the next page, there are ample opportunities for them to see causes and effects. At the same time, they will be working with mathematical concepts.

**Inference**
*What Needs to Be Done?*

Help children read the recipe for the SPICY COOKED APPLESAUCE. Explain that a recipe gives directions on how to make something to eat. Point out that a recipe does not tell a person everything she has to do and that the children will have to guess what else needs to be done.

Use as an example the cooking of the applesauce. Ask children to explain what they have to do in order to start the type of heating element being used. You may want to point out that an electric skillet must be plugged in and the correct temperature must be dialed or that gas stoves must have their pilot lights lit, be turned on, and be adjusted to the proper temperature.

Continue by asking the children what they will need to do when asked to stir the applesauce—get a spoon, make the spoon move in a circular fashion.

**Predicting Outcomes**
*How Will It All Turn Out?*

Much of mathematics involves the skill of predicting because children are often asked to estimate. How many apples it will take to make enough applesauce for all the children in the class is one example. They also can try to guess how many spoonsful will fit into the individual containers being used so each child can taste the sauce. Explain that you are asking them to make a "guess." Don't object to "wild guesses," but at the end of the estimations, let them find out the accurate answer. After they have had some practice estimating with a particular size of container, have them tell how they made their decisions about their guesses.

# SPICY COOKED APPLESAUCE

**YOU'LL NEED:**

6 apples

2 Tblsp. honey and 1 tsp. lemon rind

or

½ tsp. cinnamon and ¼ tsp. nutmeg

peeler

plastic knife

sauce pan or electric fry pan

strainer or collander

blender

grater

**WHAT TO DO**

1

Adult or child peels and cuts each apple into eight pieces.

2

Child places all pieces into a saucepan or electric fry pan.

Adult cooks apple slices on low heat (10-15 minutes) or until apples are mushy. Adult removes pan from heat

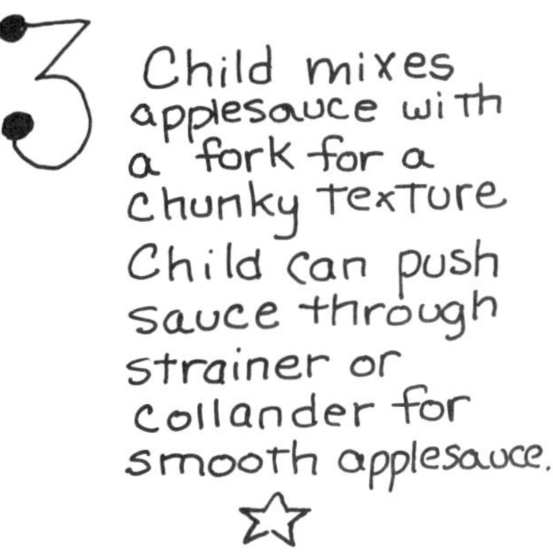

3

Child mixes applesauce with a fork for a chunky texture

Child can push sauce through strainer or collander for smooth applesauce. ☆

☆ Use a blender for extra smooth.

4

Child adds honey and lemon rind or

cinnamon and nutmeg to the cooked applesauce.

☆ Divide applesauce in half and add honey and lemon to one and cinnamon/nutmeg to the other.

# FINISH THE PATTERN

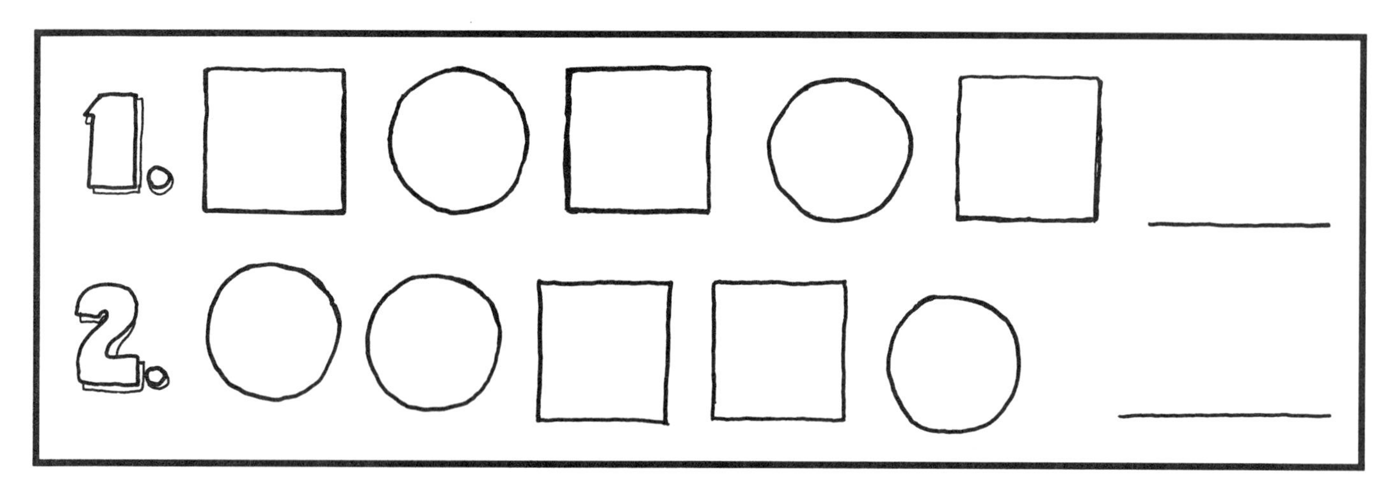

# GET THE BEAT

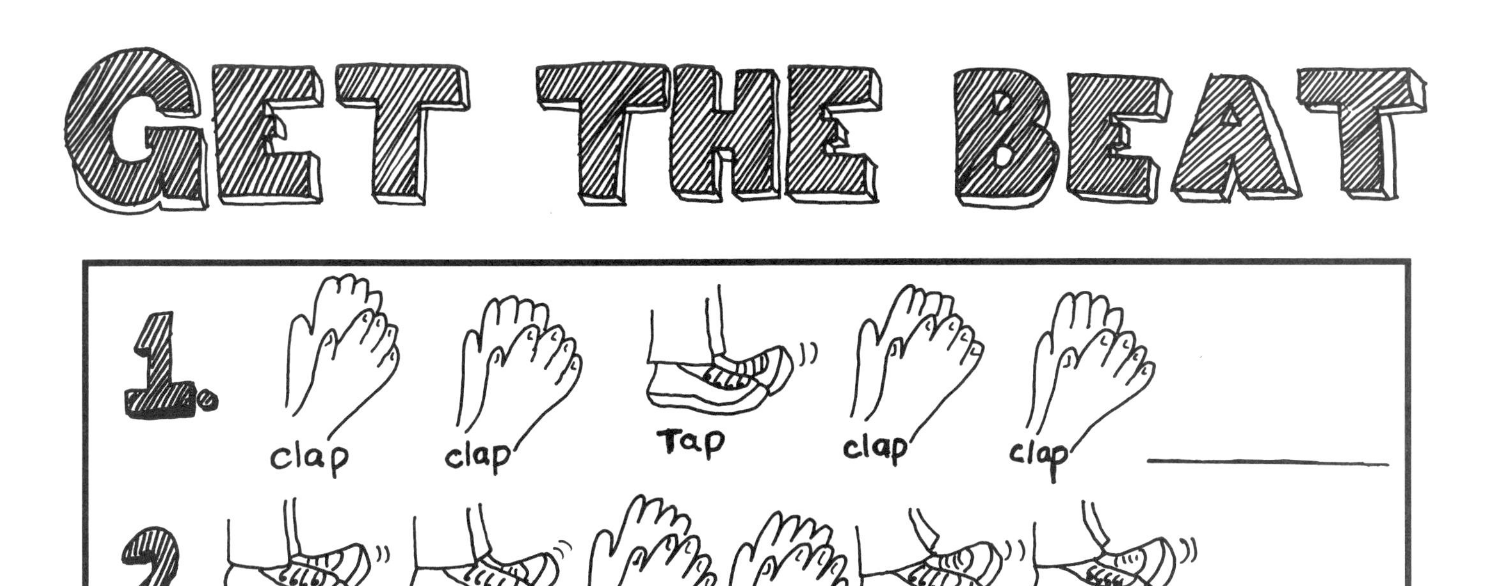
1.
clap
clap
Tap
clap
clap
2.
tap
tap
clap
clap
Tap
Tap

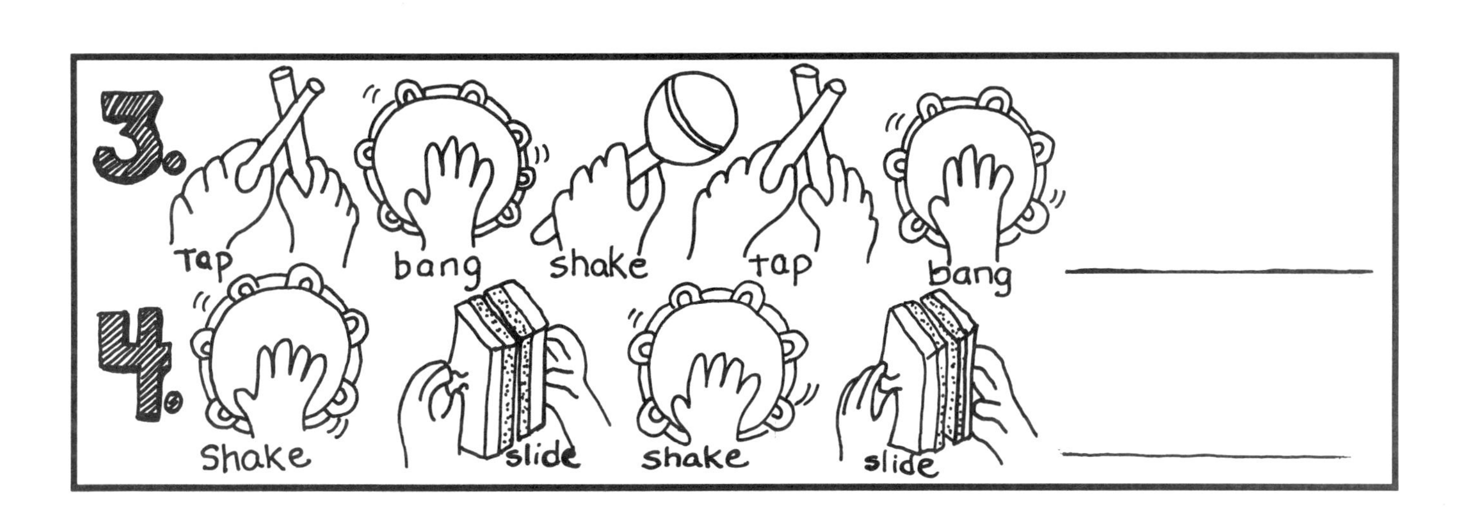
3.
Tap
bang
shake
tap
bang
4.
Shake
slide
shake
slide

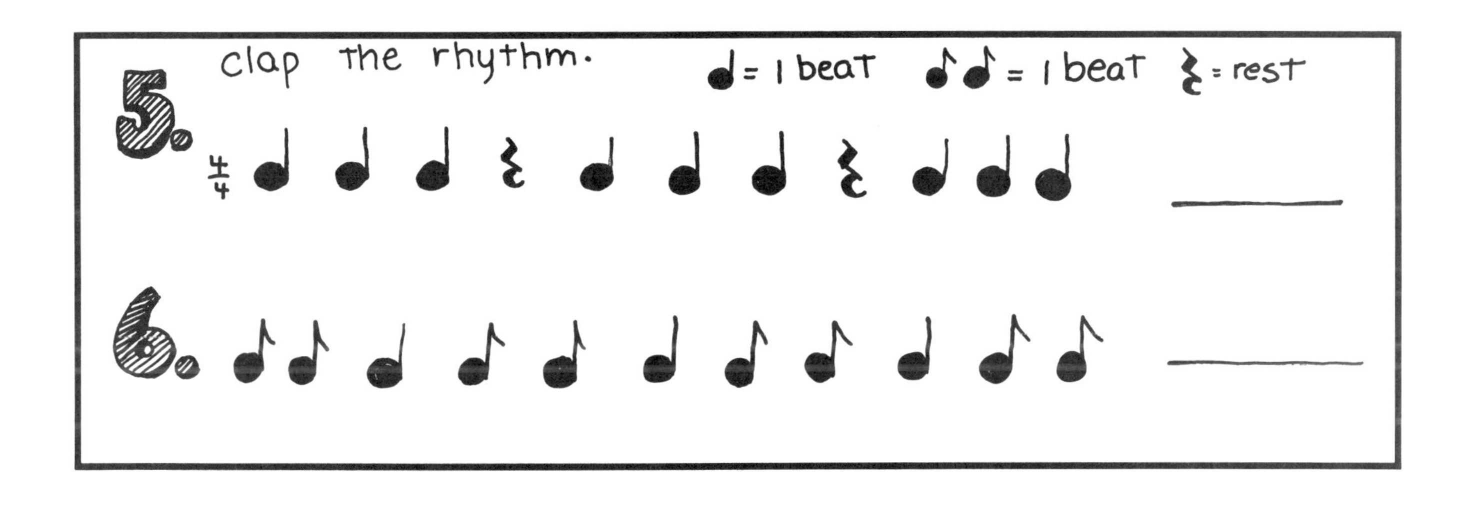
5.
clap the rhythm.
= 1 beat
= 1 beat
= rest
4/4
6.

MATH

CREATIVE THINKING

Point out that the recipe children used was entitled "SPICY COOKED APPLESAUCE." Ask them to tell what needs to be done to make it taste spicy. Help them learn how to infer what variety of spice is in a certain food. Put examples of spices out so that children will have opportunities to taste different ones. Use such spices as the following: cinnamon, nutmeg, allspice, sage, mustard, and ginger. Discuss what is being added to the applesauce.

Bring in types of food that need to be divided into serving pieces, such as a pizza, circular cake, or an apple. Let children experiment in dividing the food so that each child will be given equal pieces.

As a part of the discussion, bring out that children can use nonstandard rulers for measuring quantities. Bring in a yardstick and show them how long a yard is. Then, show how some people measure that same amount by holding one end of a piece of cloth to their nose and the other end in the fingers of the other outstretched arm. Let them also figure out how long something on the floor is by counting how many of their feet long it is. (See SELF MEASURING TOOLS on page 32.)

Ask children to think about how high their room is. Have them choose different nonstandard units that might be used to measure the height of the room. Suggest that they try to guess how many of the unit being suggested would give the vertical dimension—six boxes high; 10 drawers, and so on.

Introduce children to the concept of pairs. Let them see how many "pairs" objects they can find in their classroom. The list should include the following: scissors, eyeglasses, pants, mittens.

Let children look around the room and name containers that hold more than one item at a time, such as egg cartons, plastic rings for a six pack of juice, baskets, boxes, bookcase, and so on.

Place 20 golf balls in one container and 25 feathers in a second container that is similar in size to the first one without telling the children how many there are. Have children look at the two containers. Ask questions similar to the following.

- "What do you see in the boxes?"
- "Which box do you think has more objects in it?"
- "Which box will be heavier than the other one?"
- "Which box will be lighter than the other one?"
- "How many feathers do you think are in that box?"
- "How many golf balls do you think are in that box?"

After children have suggested answers to the questions, let them have the opportunity to examine the boxes and see if they want to change any of their answers.

# COLORS

# COLORS

**Detail/Comparison**
*Color Concentration*

Here is a game for two or three children that asks them to pay attention to a detail—color—and to compare items. You'll need cardboard and different colors of construction paper—red, yellow, blue, green, orange, purple, black, and white. Cut out 16 squares of cardboard, each of which are 3" x 3". Paste 2½" x 2½" squares of colored construction paper on each, making sure to have two squares of each color.

Mix the cards and place each one face down. Let each child take turns choosing a card and then picking up one more. Have them look at the color of each card. Explain that if the colors on the two squares are the same, the player gets to keep the pair and, if there is not a match, the player must replace both cards face down and in the same place they came from. Have children play until all pairs have been matched.

Ask children to name the color on each card as it is picked so that they will express the detail. Remind them to look at and compare the colors on the two cards they have picked. Have them tell if the two colors are the same or if they are different.

**Sequence/Comparison**
*Color Dominoes*

Most activities involve more than one skill as does this game for two or four children that enables them to make sequential patterns by matching according to similar colors. Prepare 36 heavy cardboard rectangles that are each about 1" x 3". Have available construction paper—red, yellow, blue, orange, green, purple. Draw a line in the middle of each piece of cardboard. Glue onto each cardboard on each side of the line a piece of construction paper 1" x 1½", using different color combinations. Cover the dominoes with clear plastic.

Turn all dominoes face down. Have each player choose seven of them and put the rest off to the side. Ask players to turn over their dominoes. Have the child who starts place one domino in the center of the playing area face up. Let each player in turn add one card that matches in color at one end to a card in the center. Point out that if a player cannot match at either end, that person must continue to draw from the face-down dominoes until the child can add to the sequence in the middle. Explain that each person is trying to use up all the cards placed in front of her. Have children name the sequence of the colors in the domino pattern.

Have children make patterns using the PLAY DOUGH BEADS.

**Classification**
*Color Sorting*

Individual children need to experience sorting so here they will be grouping objects using the attribute of color. Take the rectangles and squares made for Color Dominoes and Color Concentration. Make a pile of them on a table. Hold up one shape and ask children first to find all the shapes that are that same color and to place them together at one side. Help them continue to sort out one or two of the other colors. Then, have children group the remaining shapes by their colors .

# PLAY DOUGH BEADS

YOU'LL NEED:

food colors
1 cup cornstarch
2 cups baking soda
$1\frac{1}{4}$ cups water

WHAT TO DO:

**1** Combine cornstarch, baking soda, water. Stir well. Adult cooks ingredients over medium heat until they look like mashed potatoes.

**2** Remove from heat. Let set 5 minutes to cool. Knead dough ten times. Separate dough into 3 portions.

**3** Squeeze 8-10 drops each of red, blue, and yellow food color into each portion. (One will be red, one blue, one yellow.) Knead each.

**4** Roll marble-sized balls from each of the colored doughs.

**5** Push a straw through each ball or bead☆ Let beads dry overnight. Tape one end of string to make it easier to thread through dried beads.

**6** Children can string beads to make patterns using different colors.

☆ poke straw through and remove dough leaving empty hole!

# COLORS

**Cause and Effect**
*Color Experiments*

It is hard to separate art and color from children learning how and why events and results occur. Paint gives a child experience in making different shades and quantities. When it is necessary to add water to dry tempera or poster paint, children can see the effect of too little or too much of each ingredient. When the fingerpaints come out, a child, if invited to mix the paint from scratch, discovers the creative and chemical possibilities of liquid starch or wallpaper paste and the colored powder paint being mixed. The child also will learn how color can go from very dark to very light when black or white coloring is added.

Introduce the three primary colors, using crayons, tempera paint, or fingerpaint. Next, help children mix two of the three colors together to make a secondary color. Show them how to mix two other secondary colors. Then, let them experiment with adding black or white to the colors they have mixed. Help children do the activities suggested in COLORS OF MY RAINBOW.

**Inference**
*Rainbow Science*

Colors play an important part in people's lives. They help indicate changes in many scientific areas. After children have had some experiences with a certain event, they can make a guess—infer why or how it happened.

Introduce children to real rainbows. Help them notice that often on a rainy day, when the sun suddenly appears, a rainbow can be found. Have them look into the sky opposite the shining sun. Point out the dampness in the air.

Take children outside. Attach a hose to a faucet. Ask them to help you make a rainbow. Help them figure out how the hose should be used, what type of day it should be, and where the person holding the hose should be standing.

**Predicting Outcomes**
*What Will Happen When I See That Color?*

Children can use their ability to infer and their knowledge of sequence to figure out what events may occur next. Ask children to predict what will happen next in each of the following events:

- What a car will do when the traffic light in the street turns green
- What a car will do when the traffic light turns red
- When the color in the clouds changes from white to black
- When green buds appear on a bush

# COLORS OF MY RAINBOW

YOU'LL NEED:

wide paint brush

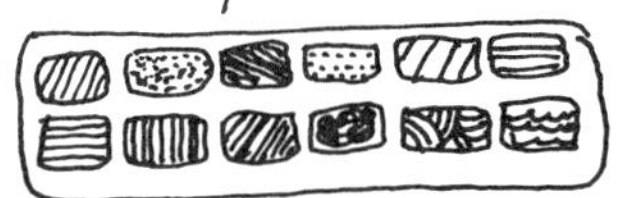

box of watercolors

8½" x 11" typing paper

water

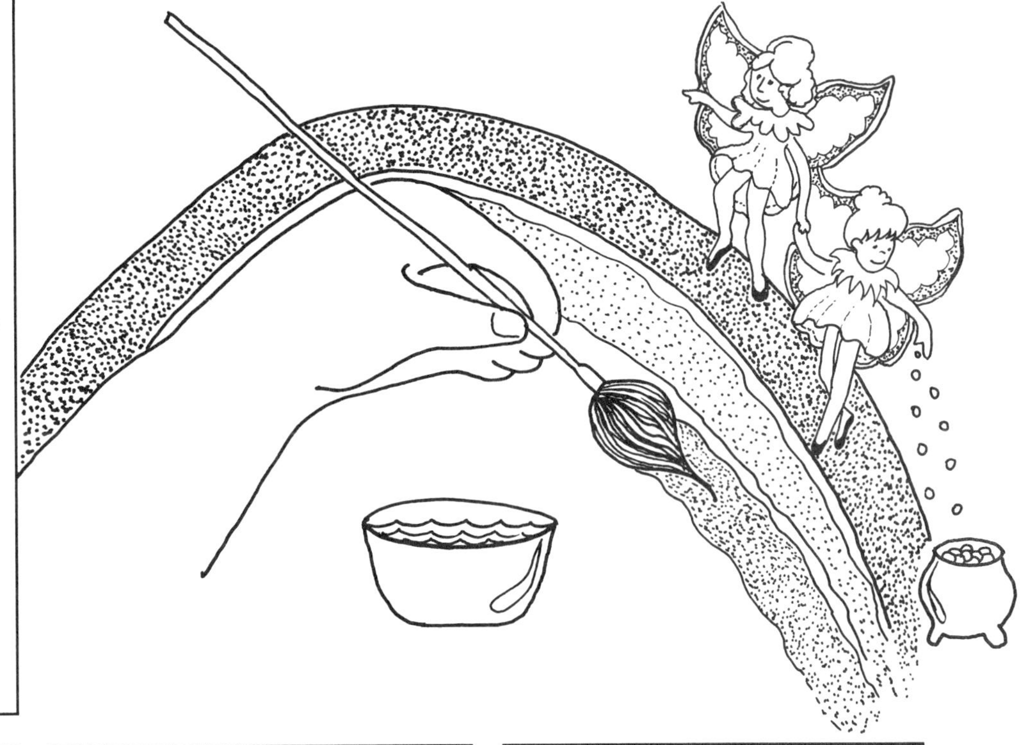

WHAT TO DO:

1. Wet paper and place on smooth surface.

2.

3. Dip brush into water and then into red paint. Make an arc with watery paint.

4. Leave about ½", then paint an arc with yellow paint.

5. Leave a ½" between the yellow paint and a blue painted arc.

6. Now watch the colors 'run.' You will see orange and green appear.

# THE FRUIT MARKET

The fruit market is a wonderful, colorful place to visit. Children can identify the various fruits by shape, size and color. Children can point out all the "yellow" or "green" fruits. They can decide if a certain color, say "red", has a similar taste and smell in different fruits. They can guess at the inside color of many of the fruits. Children can learn about red bananas, orange watermelon, 'blood' red oranges, green apples and green grapes.

Adult can reproduce these two pages for each child. The pages of fruits can be colored in according to each child's experience's "at the fruit market."

## COLORS

# CREATIVE THINKING

Ask each child first to decide what color is his favorite. Then, have children name different places and note where in that place the color can be found.

Bring in similar foods that appear in more than one color, such as apples, peppers, tomatoes, grapes. Ask "Does changing the color of a food change the taste or the way you like it?" Then, ask "Does red pepper have the same taste as a red apple?" Have children discuss what happens to the color when certain foods are cooked. You may wish to experiment and make applesauce in two different ways—using apples with and without their skins.

Have a color treasure hunt in which children have their eyes closed. Ask them to choose a color. Ask "Can you guess a color with your eyes closed if you feel it on an object?" Then, on a tray behind their backs arrange five or six items of which several are the color each child picked. Let a child feel each object and name the object and its color. Then, have them check on their guesses. Allow them time to discuss how they decided about the color of each object.

Introduce the idea of animal camouflage. You might want to use a book such as *A Color of His Own* by Leo Lionni or *We Hide, You Seek* by Jose Aruego. Then, ask questions such as the following:

- "If you were a grey elephant, where would you hide?"
- "If you were a green parrot, where would you hide?"
- "If you were a pink pig, where would you hide?"
- "If you were a blue fish, where would you hide?"
- "If you were a spotted dog, where would you hide?"
- "If you were a striped zebra, where would you hide?"

Provide children with different colors and sizes of circles, squares, triangles, and rectangles. Ask them to make some type of figures, using as many different shapes as possible. Let them add details either with small shapes or with their crayons.

Have children look around the room and at each other's clothes so that they can see different types of patterns—floral, stripes, plaids, and zigzags. Provide crayons or paints and let them figure out how to make similar patterns.

Bring out sheets of paper and jars of tempera paint. Direct children to drop blobs of one color of paint on one half of their sheets of paper. Demonstrate what is meant by one half, if necessary. Show them how to fold over the other half and press their hands over that half. Have them unfold the paper and look at the shape or shapes formed on the entire sheet of paper. Ask them to identify what each shape looks like.

# SCIENCE

# SCIENCE

**Detail**
*What Is That Object Like?*

Children should be encouraged to bring in as many senses as possible as they are faced with new experiences.

Group several objects on a tray, such as a red block, small bell, sandpaper, apple, and fresh flower. Allow time for children to observe and handle each object. Then, let children describe each item, using as many different senses and descriptive words as possible. Remind them of any sense they could have used and did not. Mention, if necessary, that they can see the color of the block but that they need to feel the block to decide if it is smooth or rough. You may wish to point out the noise that can be heard if two blocks are hit together.

**Comparison**
*Feely Game*

Children need to be able to compare real objects so that they can better understand the words used to describe the degrees of differences between objects in a similar group.

Bring in a basket of different types of fruit that children can sample. Be sure to include apples and lemons, but also have other examples: orange, pear, banana, avocado, date, grape, olive, prune, and raisin. Let different children choose two fruits and compare them using different senses, including the sense of taste. You may want to mention that some people shake melons to find out by hearing if they are ripe. Encourage the use of interesting, descriptive words such as sour, sweet, juicy, crunchy, rough. Then, play a feely game by having children put their hands behind their backs to feel what object is passed around. Start the distribution by handing out examples of fruit and letting children feel each one as it goes around the circle. At a certain point, say the word "Stop." Have each child guess what he is hiding and use as many descriptive words as possible.

**Classification**
*"Things That. . . ."*

Children need to use all their senses as they are dividing objects into the various groups in which each might be sorted.

Bring in examples of different fruits and vegetables. Let children determine different categories in which these foods could be divided, when using different senses. Children may notice that when sorting by color, fruits and vegetables can be grouped together. If necessary, help children discuss the differences in use between fruits and vegetables.

Have children make PEANUT BUTTER and then think of different ways peanut butter can be used as a food or when making other recipes.

**Sequence**
*Remember Me*

When asked to remember what objects appear in a pattern or an arrangement, point out that it helps if children study the arrangement looking at it from left to right or from top to bottom. Also, remind them to look at color patterns or other details that their senses note.

Put several objects on a tray for children to examine. Remove the tray from sight. Have children try to remember and list, tell, or draw all the objects they remember seeing.

# PEANUT BUTTER

WHAT TO DO:

Children shell and remove paper-like skin from peanuts.

2. Place 1 cup of peanuts and 1-2 tbsp. oil into blender. Blend until crunchy or smooth.

3. Add salt to taste, if desired.

Now have children brainstorm all the ways we can eat peanut butter.

# SCIENCE

**Cause and Effect**
*Why Do I Hear Sounds?*

Children hear many sounds everyday. Do they know why these sounds can be heard? You can introduce the idea of vibrations through some demonstrations. Then, you can let children produce sounds with their hands and different objects.

Put rice kernels on top of a drum. Let children tap the drum with a drumstick and watch the rice dance around on the top. Ask them to describe the way the rice moves and the noise that is made when the drum is beaten. Put a cloth between the drum and the rice and have a child hit the drum again and describe the movement of the rice and the noise.

Give children sticks, rocks, pebbles, sand, shells, and branches with leaves. Supply, also, aluminum pie plates and orange juice cans with covers. Ask them to figure out how they can make sounds with some of the items by putting them together. Then, have them try to show different types of rhythms—making them loud or soft and fast or slow. Have children work with MUSICAL CUPS to make different types of sounds.

**Inference**
*A Sound Walk*

Children hear noises everyday. Do they know what makes each sound? Often, they have to guess because sound can travel quite a distance. They need to have experiences hearing different sounds, describing what each noise sounds like, and figuring out what made that sound.

Take a walk with the children taking along a tape recorder. Have children listen for noises that you can record and tape what they suggest. When you get back to the room, play the tape and let children guess what object made each sound. See if children also can explain the operation that caused that sound to occur—such as pushing on the car horn to make it honk, stepping on a car's brakes to make a squealing noise, ringing a bell. You also may want to ask questions such as the following.

- "What are the sounds you remember the best? Why?"
- "What sounds were made by living things opening their mouths?"
- "What sounds can you imitate in some way?"

**Predicting Outcomes**
*What Kind of Noise Will This Make?*

Preschool children should be given the chance to make such things as new instruments and to figure out what kinds of sounds these instruments will make. Use the suggestion below.

Collect a large assortment of different-sized cake pans and rubber bands in different lengths and widths. Show children how to put one or more rubber bands around a pan. Then, demonstrate how each band is to be plucked. Let children then place other bands on the various cake pans. Before they start to pluck those they have placed, ask questions similar to the following.

- "Which pans do you think will make the loudest, the highest, and the lowest sounds?"
- "Which rubber bands make the loudest, highest, and lowest sounds?"

Have children do the experiments again, only this time provide them with different sizes of open boxes.

# MUSICAL CUPS

YOU'LL NEED:

3 paper cups

1 piece waxed paper

2 rubber bands

1 paper clip

1 piece of string

book

WHAT TO DO:

## 1. THE HUMMING CUP

Adult cuts the bottom out of one cup. Cover the top with piece of waxed paper. Secure with rubber band. Touch lips to paper and hum a tune. The paper vibrates and hums along.

## 2. THE GROANING CUP

Adult ties a paperclip to one end of a 12" piece of string. Make a tiny hole at the bottom of the cup and poke the string through it so that the paper clip is inside the cup. Child pulls the string that is hanging, tightly, and rubs nail along it.

## 3. THE 3 NOTE CUP

Child or adult puts the rubber band around the book. Child slips the cup under the rubber band on the book. He pushes cup to one end. He snaps the band in different places to get 3 sounds.

# city senses

Children discuss the many sights, sounds, smells, tastes and textures of the city. Older children can place symbols on city senses: 3; ; ; ; .

Put flour in a "messy area"—covered table, baby bathtub, jelly roll pan. Provide such objects or food as sifters, measuring cups, spoons, water, lentils, pasta, corn meal, rice, oatmeal. Let children feel the flour before and after it is sifted. Let them experiment sifting flour and some of the larger items. Have them also sift sand and perhaps talcum powder.

Provide children with some styrofoam packing materials, spoons, and various containers. Let them experiment so that they can see and sense the effect of static electricity. Then, add two or three inches of water to a large container. Have them discover what happens to the static electricity. Ask them to find out if the materials will float or sink. Provide strainers, sieves, and colanders as part of the experimentation. Other materials that can be tried are excelsior, "bubble" packing paper, and shredded paper.

Take children on various trips, such as to cooking areas, stores, out in the country, or into downtown or manufacturing areas. Use the following to encourage children to use their five senses.

- "What do you see here?"
- "Close your eyes and tell what your hear."
- "Do you smell anything?"
- "How does this taste?"
- "How does it feel?"
- "What does this remind you of?"

Have children decide which sense they would be using the most in the following situations:

- In the kitchen, to find out whether a casserole is done (You may wish to explain about kitchen timers.)
- In the kitchen, to find out whether the refrigerator is still working
- In a store or deli, to find out whether they sell fresh bread or spices
- In the country, to find out if there are birds and flowers nearby
- In the country or city, to find out what the trees are like
- On a bus, to find out if the road is bumpy or curvy
- On a bus or car, to find out if the directional signals are on

Provide children with homemade or rhythm band instruments or let them invent their own instruments. Let them experiment with making loud and soft noises. Ask them how to make the noise of a drum or cymbal softer or louder. Have nearby cloth or paper that could be used to dampen the noise level.

Have children find items in the room that demonstrate different sense words. You will want to have available such items as sandpaper, cotton, plastic raincoat, silk material, spices, cocoa, band instruments, timer, corn, apple, orange. Ask them to tell which sense gives them the most information.

# CHILDREN'S LITERATURE

# CHILDREN'S LITERATURE

**Detail**

*What Can You Find in This Book?*

Teachers and parents have used books for many years to broaden children's knowledge of the world. Children and adults can read the stories together and talk about them. Then, the concepts within the books can be applied to the real-life experiences of the children.

With very young children, use simple books like Leo Lionni's wordless books *What?, Who?, Where?,* and *When?* so that children can learn naming words. Then, to expand their horizons, present books such as those written by Richard Scarry. Scarry's *Best Word Book Ever* depicts objects and activities involved in many everyday events. Have the books available so that children can name or talk about what they see. Show them real-life examples. Have children name the objects and then describe the activities.

**Comparison**

*Pictures Are Worth 1000 Words*

When children are learning the skill of comparison, it is much easier for them to practice using real-life objects or activities or their pictures.

Many concept, comparison books have been written. One author that developed a number of this type is Tana Hoban. Notice, as you read the following titles, the different comparisons it is possible to depict for children: *Big Ones, Little Ones*; *Circles, Triangles, and Squares*; *Dig, Drill, Dump, Fill*; *Is It Red? Is It Yellow? Is It Blue?*; *Is It Rough? Is It Smooth? Is It Shiny?*; *Push-Pull, Empty-Full.* Through the photos, you can present many concepts or examples to children.

**Classification**

*How Can I Tell What Goes Together?*

Many concept books available can be used to help children figure out what objects "belong" in a group. As an example, the title of Richard Scarry's *Cars and Trucks and Things That Go* tells the category and two groups that fit under the "transportation" label. You can pick any concept—color, shape, number, food, transportation, size—and the subject section of the card catalog in your local library will tell you what titles are available. Choose a category and collect books that depict members of that group. Again, let children name the objects pictured. Then, let them tell the similarities that exist between items.

Children may make their own SHAPELY BOOKS after they have discussed the categories.

**Sequence**

*What Happens Next?*

A guide to children's picture books lists at least one hundred forty ABC books and at least that many counting books. Use these to introduce the simplest examples of order. From there you can go to books, such as Lucille Clifton's *Everett Anderson's Year,* that discuss the passage of seasons or ones like Gail Gibbon's *Clocks and How They Go* or Nancy Dingman Watson's *When Is Tomorrow?* in which children can talk about minutes, hours, days, and tomorrow. Then, you will want to discuss events in stories that have a definite sequence. *The Carrot Seed* by Ruth Krauss shows the growth cycle of a carrot as the hero has to tend the plant and wait some time after the seed is planted before a carrot grows.

# SHAPELY BOOKS

YOU'LL NEED:

- posterboard
- sturdy paper (typing, mimeo, ditto)
- hole punch
- assorted sizes of metal rings
- markers

WHAT TO DO:

1. Adult draws the cover shapes on posterboard and cuts out two of them.

2. Adult cuts sturdy papers in the shape of covers and places them between covers.

3. Punch 1, 2 or 3 holes (as suggested by illustrations) into all layers of book and secure with rings.

4. Use markers to decorate the covers.

5. Have children contribute a drawing for each book, discussing first the categories of things — tall, huge, tiny, long...

# CHILDREN'S LITERATURE

**Cause and Effect**
*Why Did the Little Dog Laugh?*

Children are familiar with many Mother Goose Rhymes. In some of them, the results of a person or animal's action are given—the little dog laughed "to see such sport"—so children can easily tell the cause and its effect. Others offer them opportunities to suggest some interesting effects or some funny reasons for effects to occur. Children need you to ask the questions that will spark their thinking and to allow them to make "wild" guesses.

Read some of the suggested rhymes and then ask questions similar the ones given. Children may want to act out their answers.

- *Little Miss Muffet* "Why did Miss Muffet go away?"
- *Humpty Dumpty* "Why did Humpty Dumpty fall from the wall?"
- *Jack and Jill* "What made Jack fall down and why did Jill come tumbling after?"
- *Hickory, Dickory, Dock*! "Why did the mouse run up the clock?"

**Inference**
*What's Been Left Out?*

In nursery rhymes, children have to fill in lots of gaps since the authors of the rhymes are more interested in the poetry and the rhythm than the plot. Let them make wild guesses, but ask them to explain their reasons.

Read some of the rhymes suggested below. Let children describe what took place before the event listed.

- *Little Jack Horner* Jack is sitting in a corner.
- *Old Mother Hubbard* The cupboard is bare.
- *Little Bo-Peep* Bo-Peep's sheep are lost.
- *A Diller, A Dollar* The ten o'clock scholar is arriving at noon.

**Predicting Outcomes**
*Will Boy Blue Wake Up?*

Children enjoy guessing what might or will probably happen next in stories. Since some of the nursery rhymes leave the listeners up in the air—we don't know whether Little Boy Blue ever woke up—children can come up with interesting predictions after hearing the entire rhyme and being asked questions similar to the ones below.

- *Little Boy Blue* The boy is under the haystack asleep, the sheep are in the meadow and the cow is in the corn. "Will the boy wake up? What will the sheep and cow do?"
- *Little Miss Muffet* "What could Miss Muffet do about the spider who sat down beside her?"
- *Hey, Diddle Diddle*! "What did the cow do after it jumped over the moon?"
- *Mary Had a Little Lamb* "What did Mary's lamb do while it waited for Mary?"
- *This Little Piggy* "How did the last little piggy find its way home?"
- *Little Bo-Peep* "Where did the sheep go and how will they find their way home?"
- *Humpty Dumpty* "Can Humpty be put back together again? How might you try to put Humpty Dumpty together?"

Let children make the HUMPTY DUMPTY PUZZLE so they can take it apart and put it back together.

# HUMPTY DUMPTY PUZZLE

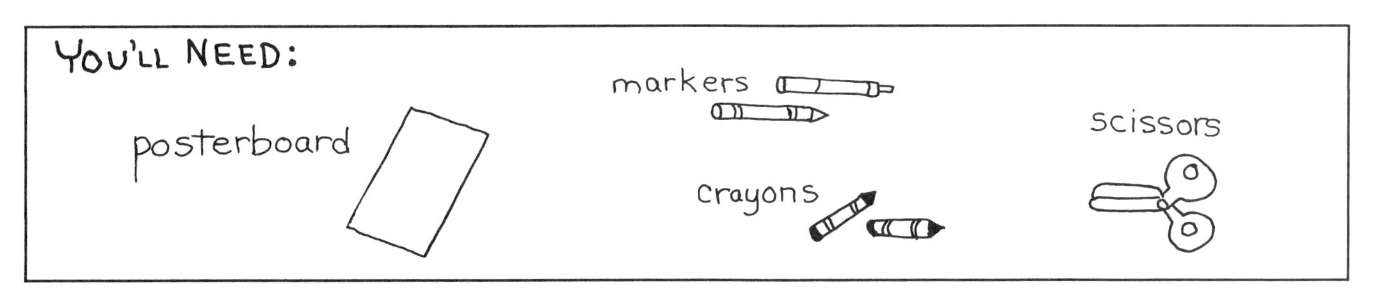


WHAT TO DO:

1. Adult cuts a large (8"X12") oval from white posterboard.

2. Children use markers to draw in features on Humpty Dumpty egg.

3. Adult (or older children) use scissors to cut egg into 8 jigsaw pieces. Child can now "put Humpty together again."

# STORY CARDS

The four scenes you see here are the settings for many hours of story telling. Each story card section suggests little scenarios that, when pieced together in one horizontal row, can make complete stories. By changing the position of the story cards, the stories can vary each time they are told.

WHAT TO DO:

1. Adult reproduces a set of story cards for each child.
2. Adult or child cuts out the four cards along the heavy, black lines.
3. Child arranges story cards to make stories. Cards can be used over and over.

Variations:

Child can draw in characters on each story card.

Child can arrange story cards in order to form a favorite story. Cards can then be glued down on paper; characters and other props permanently drawn in.

Story cards can be taped together, horizontally, and folded into a book.

## CHILDREN'S LITERATURE

# CREATIVE THINKING

Read and or have children tell familiar stories, such as *The Three Little Pigs*, *The Three Bears*, *The Three Billy Goats Gruf*, *Chicken Little*, *Millions of Cats*, and *The Little Red Hen*. Ask them to extend the stories by thinking what might happen next. For instance, ask them to decide what the two pigs whose homes were destroyed by the wolf might do. You might want to read several versions of an familiar folk tale so children can hear different endings.

Wordless books, such as Eric Carle's *Do You Want to Be My Friend?*, Helen Oxenbury's *The Shopping Trip*, or Tomi Ungerer's *A Visit to a Pond* allow children to make up events and determine the ending that they like.

Let children find pictures in magazines that depict a favorite event or draw pictures of events in their own lives. Help them record the story by writing the events as the children dictate them. Accept the statements and write them as given. You may want to encourage children to guess what the next event will be or how the situation will be resolved if there is a problem.

Pose problems using the dramatic play or the block corner. Ask children to demonstrate how the three bears might clean up their messy house after Goldilocks leaves it in a hurry or to show the best way for a pig to build a "brick" house. "Peter Rabbit" can figure out how to hide from Mr. McGregor or how to get out of the garden. In the classroom, children can build an obstacle course so that the "hare" and the "tortoise" can race again. If the hare doesn't stop to rest, will it always win? Have children try to figure out ways that would help the tortoise win.

Let children add to cumulative tales, such as *This Is the House Where Jack Lives* by Joan Heilbroner, Barbara Emberley's *Drummer Hoff*, *This Is the House That Jack Built*, or *Old MacDonald Had a Farm*.

Give children the opportunity to be imaginative by pretending to be an animal, such as a bug or an inanimate object. You might want to read something like Crockett Johnson's *Harold and the Purple Crayon*. Let them choose a color and make up some adventures for that crayon.

You can place objects in a "treasure chest" without letting the children see them. Have a child reach in, remove an item, and start a story about it. Then, ask the child to pass the object on to the next child who can then continue the story or make up one of his own. Place items like a deflated balloon, one sock, a dog leash, or a catnip mouse in the "story starter" chest.

# CELEBRATIONS

# CELEBRATIONS

**Details**
*Fun and Thinking*

Remember the enjoyable times you had years ago as you planned and participated in the many parties held for your friends or your family of dolls and stuffed animals. Do you realize that many important thinking skills you use today were developed during those early celebrations? For one thing, there were lots of details to consider.

Have children decide what type of celebration they would like to have, either a big one in which real people would be invited or a pretend one for playthings available in the room. If it is a pretend party, you may want to just observe to see what type of planning and execution the children do without any suggestions from you. If children want to include children from other rooms or adults, you may want to enter the discussions. Have present in the room props that might give children clues as to what might be needed for a party. These clues might include some of the following: dishes, silverware, food, calendars, placemats, music books, mailboxes, tea sets, empty food cartons, games, books, puppets. List on a chart the various details of the celebration that children suggest are needed.

**Comparison**
*Which Kind of Celebration Do You Like Best?*

The types of celebrations that children plan will depend in great part on the types of celebrations they have already experienced, either in their homes, in school, or in their towns.

Provide time for children to talk about different types of celebrations. These may include one or more of the following: birthday parties; holiday dinner parties with family and friends; town celebrations that include parades, pageants, or contests; meals with guests—dinners, tea parties, picnics. Let children talk about the aspects of each celebration that are alike.

Comparison also plays a part when children are arranging the details so that each guest receives the same things—food, tableware, prizes. For instance, when children set the table for their guests, they need to check that each place contains the same amount of dishes, flatware, and food.

**Classification**
*Which Kind of Celebration Will We Have?*

After children have talked about different types of celebrations, let them decide which type they want to have. Let them decide the details of that type of celebration. Point out, if needed, or help children discuss, the special requirements of a particular type of celebration—for a birthday, perhaps a cake, some candles, presents, games to play, and favors.

**Sequence**
*In What Order Should We Do Things?*

When you plan any celebration, you need to pay attention to the order in which the activities will take place. Let children decide the steps that need to be followed and the order in which they should be done. You may need to help them see the timing involved in each separate part—when they need to start preparing the food portion of the celebration or the order in which the ingredients need to be added as the cake, cookies, or pudding is being made.

Help children make HIDDEN TREASURES. Before each step, ask them to decide how long it will take to do each one.

# HIDDEN TREASURES

**YOU'LL NEED:**

2 cans of refrigerated dough (crescents)

3" circle cookie cutter

grease

1 beaten egg

water

pastry brush

rolling pin/baking sheet

fillings:
- berries
- apples
- meat balls
- cheese

**WHAT TO DO:**

1. Open the cans of dough and spread the dough flat.

2. Use the rolling pin to flatten the dough into one large sheet. Cut circles from dough with cookie cutter.

3. Choose a type of filling– either fruit or meat and cheese and place in the center of the circle.

4. Moisten the edges with water, then pull up edges, pinch together to seal in the filling completely.

5. Brush with beaten egg and bake on lightly greased cookie sheet for 18-20 min. at 375°F. Remove from cookie sheet.

6. Let cool slightly. Guess what filling is in each one! (Suggest some inappropriate fillings – see what children say.)

# CELEBRATIONS

**Cause and Effect**
*What Happens When I Change?*

There are many different kinds of effects. One occurs when children have a chance to pretend to be someone or something else. Children "become" the the characters they are pretending to be. It is helpful when a prop or costume can be added as part of their playacting. (It is also fun to have some playacting take place as part of a celebration.)

Provide opportunities for children to suggest props or costumes that they could use when they want to be certain characters by asking questions such as the ones below.

- "What clothes could we use to make us look like silly clowns?"
- "What do you need if you are going to be a king?"
- "What would you need if you were supposed to be a camel or an elephant?"
- "What type of costume can be made from large, brown paper bags?"
- "What can you do to finish a PILLOWCASE COSTUME?"

**Inference**
*What Am I Pretending?*

In a play, lots of inferences have to be drawn by both the actors and the audience because a play cannot give all the details of the story or how the actors should perform. By their costumes and their actions, the actors give clues in order to help the audience.

Provide raw materials, such as old adult clothes, aluminum foil, cardboard, oatmeal boxes, large brown bags, large pieces of fabric, pillowcases, ribbons, yarn, and rubber bands, so that children can make simple costumes or props. Let each child decide what she wants to pretend to be and devise a costume for that character. Have them keep the identity of their characters secret. Then, ask children to wear their costumes and make up dialogue and actions for a short play. Ask the others to guess who each character is.

**Predicting Outcomes**
*How Will the Play End?*

When children begin to tell what takes place in a story they are making up, they probably have not figured out how the story is going to end. If asked, they can suggest what the conclusion might be or at least the outcome of some immediate action. This should be encouraged so that children can see that different resolutions for a problem or situation can be devised.

Help children think about a story that would be appropriate for the type of celebration that is taking place. Encourage them to come up with a problem that needs to be resolved. Then, ask them to tell what will take place because the problem exists. Finally, have them decide how they would like the story to end. You may need to suggest ideas similar to the ones below at the beginning.

- "If you are a leprechaun and you lose your magic four-leaf clover, what will happen next and how will the story end?"
- "If you are an Easter Bunny and can't find any carrots to eat, what will happen next and how will the story end?"

# PILLOW CASE COSTUME

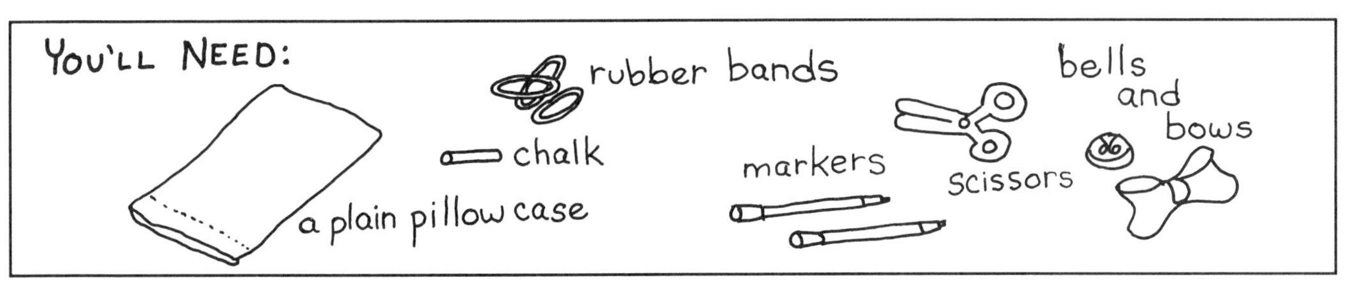

WHAT TO DO:

1. Pull up corners opposite opening and secure with rubber bands to make ears or jester hats. Use scissors to cut two arm holes.

2. While case is on child, use chalk to indicate where face is. Remove case and cut out a circle.

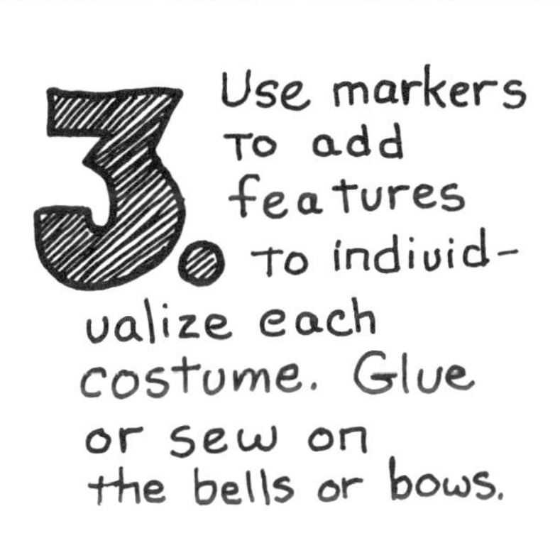

3. Use markers to add features to individualize each costume. Glue or sew on the bells or bows.

put yourself
in the picture

Pretend you are a person in this party picture. Tell what you are doing and what you are saying. What are the children celebrating? What will happen next? Set up this party scene where you are. Now pretend to have a party!

## CELEBRATIONS

Let children pretend that they are some type of bear—teddy, polar, brown. Ask them to decide what types of celebration they think bears would have. Have them decide how bears would celebrate—what they would have at each type of party in the way of food, games prizes, entertainment. Let them make some type of decorations for that party—tablecloths, centerpieces, murals, napkin rings, paper chains, paper necklaces or garlands, mobiles.

If one or more of the children bring pets, such as a cat or a bird, to the room, help them plan a "birthday" party for the pet. Have children come up with birthdates and ages for these pets. They may also want to make up similar data for some of the playthings in the room. If there are adopted children in the room, it might be desirable to have the others "adopt" a pet and prepare different types of celebrations for the adoptee.

In your town, often there will be new arrivals at a zoo, local farm, or animal refuge. Help children plan a "welcome" party for one of the newcomers. You may wish to encourage children to decide how they can tell that animal more about the town in which they now find themselves.

In planning real or pretend parties, you may want to encourage children to plan the food portion so that all the guests will receive good nutritional food that is considered part of a balanced diet. Help them learn more about good foods by making a food tree. Have a small bush or portion of a tree with branches made from construction paper on the bulletin board. Cut out hearts or some other shapes children choose. Talk about the four basic food groups—dairy, grains, meats (poultry and fish), and fruits and vegetables. Let children find examples of these foods in the pictures of magazines, paste each one on a shape, and hang on the tree. Have them choose the menu for a party from the hearts hanging on the tree.

Let children decide to celebrate something unusual. As an incentive, you might read them the story about *Alice in Wonderland* in which an "unbirthday" is celebrated. There are also at least 4,000 holidays or special days that take place each year for which special activities could be developed. A listing of these is available in *Chases's Calendar of Annual Events*, published by Apple Trees Press, Inc., Box 1012, Flint, Michigan 48501.

You may also want to encourage children to celebrate small triumphs with "small" types of festivities. Ask them to decide how to help a child celebrate "learning to tie a shoe," "losing the first tooth at school," "having a new baby at home." Ask the group to make up "celegrams"—short notes that you can write and they can decorate—so you will have some mementoes to give the honoree. Encourage each child to think of something nice to say or do for the special person. Help the honoree think of some way to say "thank you" for the "gifts" given.

# Q: WHERE CAN YOU FIND HUNDREDS OF CLASSROOM TESTED IDEAS *EACH MONTH* TO HELP YOUR CHILDREN LEARN AND GROW?

# A: IN FIRST TEACHER

Each 16 page issue of FIRST TEACHER provides you with innovative projects to make each day an exciting new adventure. We give you ideas for toymaking, games and recipes to do with young children. We take you to the world of make believe with ideas for drama and creative movement. And experts recommend the very best books for young children in FIRST TEACHER.

FIRST TEACHER has a newspaper format, but it's something to read and save. Each issue has a topical theme, so each one adds a permanent resource of projects and ideas to your school or center.

FIRST TEACHER is written by experienced caregivers, daycare directors, and nursery teachers, so it's full of tested ideas to help you guide and motivate young children

FIRST TEACHER has been read and used by over 30,000 Early Childhood teachers. Here's what one of them, Racelle Mednikow, preschool teacher for 16 years, says:

FIRST TEACHER

Vol. 6, No. 6
June, 1985

ALIVE AND GROWING

For People Who Care for Young Children

Price $2.50

WHAT'S INSIDE:
- Projects with Flowers
- Science with Plants
- An Exciting Unit on Ecology
- A Terrarium Made from a Fish Tank
- Field Trips to Learn About Growth
- A Recipe that Grows
- And, Lots More!

*"What a pleasure to be provided with well written, resourceful and usable ideas that can be interjected into our everyday curriculum and be of true value to each of our teachers!"*

*"Thank you so much for this delightful, informative newspaper."*

**Subscribe today!** Don't miss another month of ideas, projects, and activities.

| SUBSCRIBE TODAY AT THIS SPECIAL INTRODUCTORY PRICE! **$17.95** ($6.05 OFF THE REGULAR PRICE) | **Write to:** FIRST TEACHER<br>Box 29<br>60 Main Street<br>Bridgeport, CT 06602<br>**Or call:** 1-800-341-1522<br>(8AM - 9PM Mon. - Fri.<br>9AM - 5PM Sat.) |
|---|---|